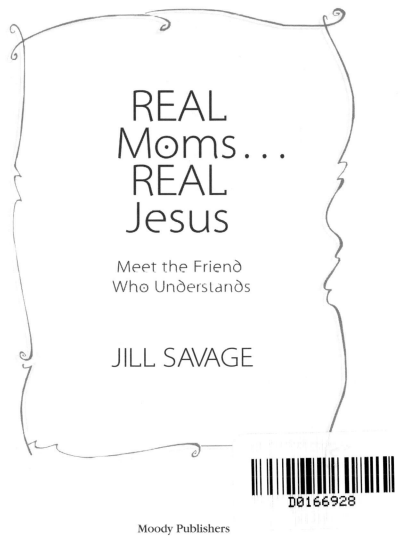

REAL
Moms...
REAL
Jesus

Meet the Friend
Who Understands

JILL SAVAGE

D0166928

Moody Publishers
CHICAGO

© 2009 by
JILL SAVAGE

Unless otherwise noted, Scripture quotations are taken from the *Holy Bible, New International Version*®. NIV®. Copyright © 1973, 1978, 1984 by International Bible Society. Used by permission of Zondervan. All rights reserved.

Scripture quotations marked NLT are taken from the *Holy Bible, New Living Translation,* copyright © 1996, 2004. Used by permission of Tyndale House Publishers, Inc., Wheaton Illinois 60189, U.S.A. All rights reserved.

Scripture quotations marked THE MESSAGE or MSG are from *The Message,* copyright © by Eugene H. Peterson 1993, 1994, 1995. Used by permission of NavPress Publishing Group.

Scripture quotations marked NKJV are taken from the *New King James Version.* Copyright © 1982 by Thomas Nelson, Inc. Used by permission. All rights reserved.

Scripture quotations marked NASB are taken from the *New American Standard Bible*®, Copyright © 1960, 1962, 1963, 1968, 1971, 1972, 1973, 1975, 1977, 1995 by The Lockman Foundation. Used by permission. (www.Lockman.org)

Published in association with the literary agency of Alive Communications, Inc., 7680 Goddard St., Suite 200, Colorado Springs, CO 80920. www.alivecommunications.com

Cover design: Julia Ryan | www.DesignByJulia.com
Cover photo: © JupiterImages Corporation
Interior design: Julia Ryan |www.DesignByJulia.com
Images/Photos: © 2008 www.iStockphoto.com, © 2008 JupiterImages Corporation

Library of Congress Cataloging-in-Publication Data

Savage, Jill, 1964-
  Real moms ... real Jesus : meet the friend who understands / Jill Savage.
     p. cm.
  Includes bibliographical references.
  ISBN 978-0-8024-8361-4
  1. Mothers—Religious life. 2. Jesus Christ—Person and offices. 3. Spirituality. I. Title.
  BV4529.18.S26 2009
  248.8'431—dc22

                              2008037009

We hope you enjoy this book from Moody Publishers. Our goal is to provide high-quality, thought-provoking books and products that connect truth to your real needs and challenges. For more information on other books and products written and produced from a biblical perspective, go to www.moodypublishers.com or write to:

Moody Publishers
820 N. LaSalle Boulevard
Chicago, IL 60610

5 7 9 10 8 6

Printed in the United States of America

You are my friends when you
do the things I command you. . . .
I've named you friends because I've let you in on
everything I've heard from the Father.

Jesus Christ

*This book is dedicated to my children
Anne, Evan, Erica, Kolya, and Austin.
May my friendship with God lead the way
to your friendship with God.
And may you never forget that you
have a Savior who understands.*

CONTENTS

Acknowledgments

A book is never the work of one person. It is a result of the combined efforts of dozens of people. With that in mind, special thanks goes to:

. . . my prayer partners who faithfully lift me up to the Lord. Special thanks to Becky for your fabulous communication with my prayer team.

. . . my manuscript readers MarLo, Diane, Julie, and Megan. Thank you for taking the time to read and give me valuable feedback. Diane, thank you for helping with research and keeping me as organized as possible. You're a gift!

. . . my Hearts at Home team. Without you, this book would not exist. Thank you for your tireless work to encourage, educate, and equip women in the profession of motherhood.

. . . my literary agent, Beth Jusino at Alive Communications, and the Moody Publishers team. Thank you all for believing in the message of this book. It's been a pleasure working with you.

. . . my incredible family. Thanks, kids, for being willing to have a few more nights of frozen pizza than usual. You guys are the best kids a mom could ask for!

. . . my husband, Mark. It's been twenty-five years of learning, loving, and leading together. I love you more today than the day I said, "I do." Thank you for your love, your support, and your willingness to pick up the slack in those last few days before a deadline!

. . . my Savior, Jesus Christ. You've transformed my heart and renovated my life. Thank You for Your unending grace, Your perfect love, and Your life-changing truth. Most of all, I'm thankful that You are truly a Friend who understands.

You Are Not Alone

*H*ave you ever felt alone? Maybe you've convinced yourself that "nobody's ever felt this way before." Have you longed for a friend who understands?

Every mom has experienced those feelings—and more. She's felt isolated, alone, weary, and overwhelmed. But the truth is you are *not* alone. By turning the pages of this book you'll meet two friends who understand what your life is like.

The first friend you'll meet is me . . . a fellow traveler on the journey of motherhood. I'm glad to make your acquaintance! Five children and over thirty years of marriage have given me the opportunity to make plenty of mistakes, but learn more about myself and my God than I ever thought possible. Since 1994 I've been encouraging moms through the ministry of Hearts at Home (www.hearts-at-home.org) an organization designed to encourage, educate, and equip women in the profession of motherhood. The book you're holding is a Hearts at Home resource—one of many we've designed just for moms like yourself.

I doubt you picked up this book to meet me, however. You were most likely drawn to the other Friend you're going to get to know as you read through this book: Jesus Christ, God in the flesh. As we'll discover together, Jesus was fully God, yet fully man. It is His human experiences we'll focus on over these pages to discover new perspectives about this Friend who really understands us.

Maybe you've never thought about Jesus that way. I certainly didn't until several years ago. That's when I decided to read the books of the Bible that are a biography of Jesus' life: Matthew, Mark, Luke, and John. As I read, the stories of Jesus' life came alive to me and I began to see Him in a different light. I'm so excited to be able to share with you the new perspective I discovered!

If you're comfortable with the Bible, join me in looking at Jesus in a new and exciting way. If you've never been much of a Bible reader, let this easy-to-read book introduce you to the exciting truths found in God's Word.

While it's not necessary for reading this book, if you don't have a Bible, you might want to get one. I think you'll be intrigued to read some on your own. If you are unfamiliar with the different versions available, I primarily use three versions in these pages: NIV stands for *New International Version*, NLT stands for *New Living Translation*, and *The Message* (also marked MSG in the text) is a paraphrased Bible that uses more common, everyday language. If no version is cited, the reference comes from the NIV.

When choosing a version of the Bible for yourself, try reading the same verse from several different versions and see which version is easiest for you to understand. Sometimes a study Bible is helpful, too, because it provides notes and background information that can be helpful for understanding what you read.

This book is designed for individual and group use. If you want to use this as a study resource for your moms group, you'll find the leader's guide in the back of the book very helpful. If you're reading the book by yourself, feel free to join me on my blog for discussion and more encouragement. You can find me online at www.jillsavage.org and www.HeartsatHome.org.

There are two elements to this book that I believe you'll find helpful. Before each chapter you'll find Perspective. Each Perspective is designed to present a brief picture from Jesus' life and how His experience relates to our experience as a mom. The Perspective pieces are also designed to acquaint you with talking with God and reading His Word. If you choose to read the suggested Bible chapters with each Perspective, you will have read the entire book of Matthew by the time you finish the book.

The chapters in this book look at the character of Christ. The Bible says that we are to become more like Jesus Christ as we mature in our faith. Each chapter will explore not only Jesus' experience on this earth, but how He lived His life as well. By looking at how Christ lived His life, we will discover a template for our own lives.

Want to know you're not alone? Tired of feeling like no one understands? Look no further. With the turn of a page, you *will* find a Friend who understands.

Perspective

How can God understand?

J slipped out of bed in the wee hours of the morning. My night-owl body rarely sees 5:00 a.m., but on this particular morning I had awakened and could not go back to sleep. I donned my robe and slippers and walked gingerly down the hall of our hundred-year-old farmhouse, placing each step right next to the baseboard—a technique I've perfected to minimize the creaks of our old wooden floor. A desperate mom does desperate things to assure her children stay asleep, even if it means walking down the hallway as if she is balancing on two parallel tightropes.

It felt as if there wasn't enough of me to go around. With one child in preschool, one in grade school, one in junior high, and one in high school, I was trying to meet the diverse needs of our then four children in four different seasons of life. I longed for quiet and craved solitude.

Once I made it to the main level of the house, I fixed myself a cup of tea, grabbed my Bible, and nestled into my favorite recliner rocker.

This was my time with my best Friend . . . Jesus. I'd had "snacks" with Him, but I was craving a meal . . . uninterrupted time to talk.

Not more than two minutes went by before I heard the footie pajamas coming across the dining room floor. Austin peeked around the doorway and inquired in his sleepy, four-year-old voice, "Mom, were you waiting for me?"

You see, Austin and I had a morning routine of spending our first few minutes out of bed snuggling in the rocker and talking about our day. And he was just sure that's what I was up so early for!

Jesus understands my life and my frustrations. He, too, was interrupted as He went about His daily activities.

I remember one story in the Bible when Jesus was traveling from Judea to Galilee. The trip took Him through a place called Samaria. "Jesus, worn out by the trip, sat down at the well. It was noon. A woman, a Samaritan, came to draw water." And from there a conversation ensued and Jesus spoke truth into the Samaritan woman's life. (Read the story in John 4:1–26.) Jesus was on His way to Galilee with a goal in mind when life happened and He had an opportunity to encourage someone along the way.

Then there was the time that Jesus was entering Jericho on his way to Jerusalem. He happened upon a tax collector named Zacchaeus who wanted so badly to see Him that he climbed a sycamore tree in order to catch a glimpse of this man he'd heard so much about. When Jesus passed by the tree, He called to Zacchaeus and told him that they needed to spend time together. (See Luke 19:1–10.) Again, He was goal oriented, but life happened.

Ministry for Jesus was the person standing in front of Him: the woman at the well, a tax collector, someone who needed healing, someone who had a question for Him.

Ministry for you and for me is the same. It's the people standing in front of us: our husband, our children, friends, neighbors, and even complete strangers at times.

I like to call what I do every day as a mom "the ministry of availability." More often it feels like the "ministry of interruptions." But my daily experiences are similar to the experiences Jesus had when He walked upon this earth. He was in high demand. I'm in high demand. He was interrupted dozens of times a day. I'm interrupted dozens of times a day. He was asked a million questions. It feels like I'm asked a million and one questions a day! Talking with Jesus is like having a Friend who understands!

After a weary sigh, I lifted Austin into my lap and replied to his question: "Mommy is talking with Jesus, but you can sit here with me if you'd like. I love our snuggle time each morning." Ministry for me is the person standing in front of me—and at that moment it was my four-year-old son.

Pray . . .

Thank you, God, for sending Your Son to live on this earth.
Thank You for giving us a Savior who understands the human
experiences. Help me to grow to know You better and to trust
Jesus as my Friend and my Savior. And help me to reframe what
I do every day as a mom—seeing the interruptions as opportunities
rather than frustrations. Grow in me a servant's heart that
ministers to whoever is standing in front of me.

(Feel free to continue journaling your thoughts to God.)

How often I grow frustrated by interruptions, God! Shift my perspective and please help me to be more like You. Even when I'm the most spent, help me to serve and minister to those right in front of me. Thank You for NEVER being frustrated by my interruptions or questions!

Discover . . .

Read chapters 1 and 2 in the book of Matthew.
This will introduce you to Jesus' life on this earth. Before you read,
ask God to show you the human side of Jesus.

TRUTH . . .

We don't have a priest [Jesus] who is out of
touch with our reality. He's been through weakness and
testing, experienced it all—all but the sin. So let's walk
right up to him and get what he is so ready to give.
Take the mercy, accept the help.

HEBREWS 4:15–16 (THE MESSAGE)

CHAPTER 1

DISCOVER GOD'S TRUTH:

JESUS SERVED

The Truth about Serving

*I*t must have been the end to a long, hot day. Having been on their feet for the better part of the day, the evening meal was a much-needed time of rest and refreshment for Jesus and His friends. It signaled the end of work and the beginning of a time of community. I'm sure the conversation centered on the events of the day, the miracles they had witnessed, and the people they had come in contact with.

Unnoticed by the others, Jesus "got up from the supper table, set aside his robe, and put on an apron. Then he poured water into a basin and began to wash the feet of the disciples, drying them with his apron" (John 13:4–5 MSG).

Peter protested, but Jesus continued. Jesus' companions must have looked at one another with amazement and the murmuring around the table probably sounded like the buzz of busy bees.

"What is He doing? Why is He doing the job of a servant?" they asked one another.

Jesus finished washing each friend's feet, and then He removed the apron, put His robe back on, and went back to His place at the table. "Then he said, 'Do you understand what I have done to you? You address me as "Teacher" and "Master," and rightly so. That is what I am. So if I, the Master and Teacher, washed your feet, you must now wash each other's feet. I've laid down a pattern for you. What I've done, you do'" (John 13:12–15 MSG).

It was the ultimate act of servant leadership. Most important, it set the example for how we're to live our everyday lives.

Servant Leadership

Every day you and I have the opportunity to practice servant leadership. The profession of motherhood is about meeting the needs of others, caring for them physically, emotionally, and relationally. It requires a giving heart, a selfless spirit, and a strong sense of identity to serve generously.

Most moms don't think of themselves as a leader. But that's what a parent is. They are the leader of their children. Jesus described Himself as "Master" and "Teacher." We are that to our children. Certainly they don't call us "master," but a master is defined as "a person whose teachings others accept and follow." [1]

Let's be honest: my children don't always accept my teachings, but for the most part they do follow them. And "teacher"—I doubt any of us would disagree with that. Mothers are natural teachers. We are imparting wisdom, giving direction, and helping our children learn about their world every day.

Jesus' titles of Master and Teacher were titles of authority. He was their leader. But in the humbling act of washing His pupils' feet, He balanced authority leadership with servant leadership. He

1. http://dictionary.reference.com

brought alive Matthew 20:16, "So the last will be first, and the first will be last." So is that saying that by being a servant we can become an even more influential leader in our kids' lives? That's exactly what Jesus said. I know . . . it's hard to fathom. It's mind-blowing. It's countercultural. And it's Christlike.

What's a Mom to Do?

They say with kids more is caught than taught. What they see us do is far more important than what we tell them to do. They follow our example and grow up to be more like us than we'd sometimes like them to be. They "catch" our good and our bad.

Many of the things I do as a mother I do because I'm following the example of my mother. But she's not the only example I have to follow. For those of us who believe in Jesus Christ, we have His example to follow. He lived to give and He died serving. He was the King of Kings and the Lord of Lords, but He lived the humble life of a carpenter. He had the title of all titles: the Lord God Almighty, but He didn't force Himself on anybody, nor did He require that people bow down and worship Him. Instead He shared meals with tax collectors and slept in the wilderness. He spent time with the "least of these" and showed love to the unlovely. Now that's a hard act to follow.

We read in John 13:15–16 (NLT), "I have given you an example to follow. Do as I have done to you. I tell you the truth, slaves are not greater than their master. Nor is the messenger more important than the one who sends the message." Jesus asks us to follow His example. We're not perfect. We won't do it exactly right. But we're called to become more Christlike every day. Personally I'm thankful to have a God who not only says, "Do as I say," but also, "Do as I do." He led by example and showed us that it is doable.

Our human nature struggles with the concept of "being last." We often give to get. We serve with the expectation of being served in return. Yet the very nature of mothering responsibilities slowly erodes that sense of entitlement and selfishness that we often bring into adulthood. Once a child grabs hold of our heart, we find a generosity in us like we've never experienced before. The sense of entitlement fades away and we learn to work harder than we've ever worked in our lives. We go without sleep and forget to eat. We give even when it feels like we have nothing left to give. Sometimes all we receive back from a cranky baby is a headache and from a rebellious teenager a heartache. That doesn't feel like much return for all the time, energy, and love we've given so freely.

Before we know it, we can begin to feel taken advantage of. And if we aren't careful, we lose valuable perspective. This is where serving has to have balance—and to learn about that balance we need to again follow the example of our Friend who understands.

Serve with a Curve

The Bible is full of stories of Jesus' busy life. He traveled, He spoke, He healed, He listened, He shared, He taught; and then He went to bed and did it all over again the next day. Yet even in the midst of a life of service, He knew that if you give freely you have to curve around and receive freely as well. Serving with a straight line (giving and not receiving) may result in burnout, bitterness, and sheer exhaustion.

The Bible tells us, "Jesus often withdrew to lonely places and prayed" (Luke 5:16). This was Jesus' primary time of receiving. He refueled His emotional and spiritual fuel tank by spending time with God. He stepped away from the spotlight to pray and get His direction from His Father.

I once read that Susanna Wesley (1669–1742), the mother of nineteen, would pull up her hoop skirt over her head to find a moment to pray. Susanna was the mother of John Wesley, considered the founder of the Methodist Church, and Charles Wesley, the great hymn writer. That's a mom who understood her need to pull up to the spiritual filling station so she had the love, perspective, and energy to serve her very large family. You and I need to do the same.

We'll talk about prayer more in depth in a later chapter, but let's look at spending time with God as an essential part of serving. Serving is giving. Spending time with God is receiving. You and I need to receive from God hope, truth, love, encouragement, perspective, and value. Spending time with Him will fill our tank so that we serve out of the overflow of what God has filled us with. God confirms this in 2 Corinthians 1:3–5: "God . . . comforts us in all our troubles, so that we can comfort those in any trouble with the comfort we ourselves have received from God. For just as the sufferings of Christ flow over into our lives, so also through Christ our comfort overflows." Also in 2 Corinthians 9:10–11 (MSG), "This most generous God . . . gives you something you can then give away, which grows into full-formed lives, robust in God, wealthy in every way, so that you can be generous in every way, producing with us great praise to God." When we spend time with God, we fill up until we are overflowing and it is out of the overflow that we are able to serve others.

How do we receive from God? There are two ways: talking to Him (prayer) and reading His instruction manual (the Bible). Don't worry about formalities here; God just wants you to talk

Spending time with Him will fill our tank so that we serve out of the overflow of what God has filled us with.

with Him. What are your struggles? Tell Him. What are you angry about? Tell Him. What is tripping you up in your relationships? Tell Him. What are you thankful for? Tell Him. What fears do you have? Tell Him. What are your hopes and dreams for the future? Tell Him. God just wants to hear our heart. He already knows our needs, but He longs for us to trust Him and invite Him into our daily life.

> What are your hopes and dreams for the future? Tell Him. God just wants to hear our heart.

Just like Jesus, I need to "withdraw from the crowds" to pray. Realistically, He probably sat on a rock in the desert to pray and I most often sit on a toilet in the bathroom (with the lid down, of course!). Seriously, the bathroom is sometimes the only place where a mom can find a few minutes of quiet. So use what you have! Keep a Bible and a notebook in the bathroom to read a few nuggets of truth and journal your prayers. Or just close the door, take a couple of deep breaths to quiet your mind, and talk with the Lord for a few moments.

If you can get up a few minutes before your family to spend time with God, you will fill up your tank before you start serving. Even just five or ten minutes can make a huge difference in a mom's day. I've always struggled with this myself, because I'm more of a night owl than an early bird. But when I've managed to make it happen, I notice a huge difference in my ability to care for my family.

My friend Becky writes Scripture on index cards and places the cards all over the house: on her bathroom mirror, on the refrigerator, next to the computer, on the dash of her car . . . anywhere she will be so that she can be reminded of God's truth for her life. Any time we read God's Word—even if it's one verse at a time—we fill up our tank so we can serve out of our overflow.

Receiving The Serve

When Mark was attending Bible college and we were struggling to make ends meet, we were approached by the pastor of our church one Sunday. He walked up to Mark, extended his hand for a handshake and placed a $100 bill in his pocket. Mark immediately tried to give the money back, but Don wouldn't allow him to give it back. Finally Don said something neither Mark nor I have ever forgotten. He said, "Don't ever deny me the opportunity to serve my Lord." We were powerfully affected by Don's words and we quickly learned another aspect of serving. If someone serves, then someone else has to receive.

Most of us struggle with receiving. We either see it as a sign of weakness to have someone help us, or we hate to cause another person any inconvenience. But an important part of serving is also graciously receiving when God asks someone else to serve.

As moms, most of us fall easily into the "I'll take care of it myself" mind-set. When someone asks if they can help, we respond, "No, I think I'm doing okay." We labor alone, often ending up emotionally overwhelmed or physically exhausted. A mother who does everything for the family and expects nothing from them will raise children who grow up and have no sense of responsibility. We need to invite our children to serve right alongside of us. And sometimes we even need to allow them to serve us. That's a challenge for most of us, but a very important part of modeling a balanced picture of serving.

Jesus also models the receiving side of serving. He allowed others to occasionally make dinner for Him. He let a woman pour perfume on His feet and wipe His feet with her hair. He permitted the disciples to steer a boat He was in so He could sleep. He gave

Himself completely, but He balanced the serving He did with allowing others to serve Him, as well. It's a pattern set for us to follow.

How do we apply this to everyday life in the trenches of motherhood? Consider these possibilities:

- When your husband says "How can I help you?" don't brush away his question, but invite him to join you in whatever you are doing.

- If your neighbor comes over while you're making a fruit salad for the neighborhood cookout, ask her to help you cut up the strawberries.

- Rather than making dinner alone for your family night after night, ask your children to help you with age-appropriate tasks. A preschooler can help set the table; a grade-schooler can help clean vegetables or make a salad. A teenager is fully capable of being in charge of planning and preparing one meal each week.

- When your mother-in-law comes over and takes it upon herself to clean your kitchen, be grateful for the help rather than offended by her actions. Thank her for her servant heart and graciously receive the gift.

- The next time you are sick and a girlfriend calls you during the day and asks if she can bring you dinner . . . say yes!

A Servant Heart

In today's me-first society, having a servant heart can be considered countercultural. But the joy of serving others offers an experience like none other. Because we are made in the image of God, we are designed to serve.

The profession of motherhood is about caring for the needs of those around us. But as Christ showed us, we have to both give and receive. And we have to serve out of the overflow of our heart rather than our emptiness. There is great strength and beauty in serving our family, friends, and neighbors, and allowing them to serve us. Christ served freely and we are called to do the same!

Jesus, Thank You for showing me the balance of serving. Help me to serve with a right heart and to recognize the gift I offer when I serve. Most important, though, help me to learn to receive. It's so hard to let others serve me, yet I know that's part of the deal, too! Let me both give and receive. As I hang with You, Lord, and learn more about You, help me to be more like You every day.

"By being a servant, we can become an even more influential leader in our kids' lives."

REMIND ME, God... to give to others I have to fill myself first with You. Teach me, please, how to serve and receive generously and graciously.

Perspective

Help! Everyone wants a piece of me.

Erica was so unhappy. "Uncomfortable" was the only word to describe this third child of mine. We never experienced colic with the first two babies, but this one had been crying nonstop for nearly six months. My two older children were six and four and still needed a lot of my attention. On one particular day I remember feeling like I had a baby attached to my breast and a preschooler attached to each leg the entire day. I finally tucked everyone into bed for the night and I made a beeline for my own bed . . . only to find a husband with a gleam in his eye!

I wanted to scream, "If one more person touches this body, I'll lose it!"

Let's face it. When we launch into the journey of motherhood, it takes a physical toll on us. If you give birth, you lose all sense of modesty once labor sets in. Every part of your body is pushed, pulled, looked at, and touched in ways you would have never imagined possible. Once that beautiful little one is placed in your arms, he begins rooting for his first meal and your breasts suddenly have a new job.

Maybe you came into motherhood through adoption. Still, children have to be carried as infants. As they enter the toddler and preschool years they seem to think you are a moving piece of playground equipment—jumping, hanging, and climbing on you nonstop.

We can't forget Dad in all of this. In the midst of all the "little people" demanding their needs be met, Dad can easily move from his well-earned place on the top of the priority list to right under "feed the dog" at the bottom of the list. That's not the way it should be . . . it just happens if we're not careful.

When Jesus lived on this earth, it seemed that everyone wanted a piece of Him. There are many stories in the Bible that show people wanting Jesus' time and His touch. Some waited patiently for their turn and others pushed their way through the crowd to simply touch the hem of His garment. One particular story about a woman who was desperate to touch Jesus comes to mind. The Bible says she had been bleeding for twelve years and she believed Jesus could heal her. She pushed her way through the crowd and was able to just touch His clothing. Because of her faith, she was healed. (Read about her in Matthew 9:20–22.)

Jesus' experience on this earth is very similar to ours as mothers. Our family wants our time and our touch. Some wait patiently (like a weary husband) and others demand their way (like a screaming baby). Jesus was in high demand, and as mothers we are in high demand, as well.

Jesus modeled for us how to handle the demands that are placed upon us. His strategies included prayer and knowing how to find quiet moments in the midst of the chaos. We'll explore those more in the coming pages, but for now simply focus on the fact that He understands. He gets it. He knows what it feels like for everyone to want a piece of you.

Pray . . .

Thank you, God, for the diary of Your life in the Bible.
Thank You for the stories about everyone wanting to touch You
and spend time with You. You really do understand me and how
it feels like everyone wants a piece of me. Help me to find Your peace
in the midst of mothering. Help me to keep my eyes on You as I
accomplish the tasks of motherhood. In Jesus' name, Amen.

Take a few minutes to talk with Him some more.
Don't worry, He's not looking for formality—He just wants you
to share your heart and what's on your mind.

I'm sorry, Jesus, for doing a very poor job handling the neediness of others in the past. Please forgive me for not dealing with chaos as You did, and please help me to be more like You and to find Your peace when it seems like everyone needs my attention.

Discover . . .

Read Matthew chapters 3 and 4. Ask God to show you
a different side of Jesus than you've ever seen before.

TRUTH . . .

So, my dear Christian friends, companions in following this call to the heights, take a good hard look at Jesus. He's the centerpiece of everything we believe, faithful in everything God gave him to do.

HEBREWS 3:1–2 (THE MESSAGE)

CHAPTER 2

DISCOVER GOD'S TRUTH:
JESUS WORSHIPED

The Truth about Worship

he crowd cheered as the teams took the field. The fans visually showed support with homemade signs, official team apparel, clothing colors, and even painting their skin with the appropriate colors. Every time their team scored, the supporting crowd rose to their feet with a roar. They cheered, jumped up and down, and did all kinds of crazy things that are considered "normal" at a football game.

The fans are devoted to their team. They respect, honor, and adore the players and the coaches. And although we don't usually use the word "worship" to describe football fans, that is exactly what they are doing. They are giving worth to something they love . . . and that is what worship is all about.

Understanding Worship

Most of our children have had a "match the shape" toy at some time. This is usually a ball or a box that has different-shaped pieces that will only fit through the correspondingly shaped hole. It teaches the child different shapes and helps develop eye-hand coordination. But that same toy provides a visual analogy for us, as well. You see, our lives are very much the same way. There's a God-shaped hole in each of our hearts. Whether we realize it or not, it's there. And whether we realize it or not, we're always trying to fill it.

There's a God-shaped hole in each of our hearts . . . we're always trying to fill it.

Some of us try to fill it with food. Some of us try to fill it with relationships—expecting our husband, our children, or a friend to be something they can't be. Some try to fill it with work, school, degrees, or titles that make us feel good about ourselves. Some try to fill it with shopping or hobbies. Some of us try to fill that hole with perfectionism—an elusive sedative that gives a false sense of security and skyrocketing expectations for others.

Every time we try to fill that hole with something other than God we build an idol: a false god in our life. The more we pursue the false god, the more we turn our worship (deeming something worth our time and energy) away from the Creator and more toward the created. And we'll always come up short every time.

When we understand the God-shaped void inside of us and we allow God to fill His rightful place in our hearts and our lives, we move from a me-perspective to a God-perspective. When we do this, we are freed up to recognize that God's truth and His ways are the only things worth our time and energy. And we also learn that our everyday activities, when done with a God-perspective, are an act of worship that really touches the heart of God.

Redefining Worship

Culturally we've come to associate the word "worship" with church. We go to church to worship God. Or we say that we are going to a "worship service." In reality, we go to church to participate in corporate worship. This is where we gather with other believers to worship God together once or twice a week. This type of worship is an important part of the journey of faith, but it was never meant to solely define worship.

When you get right down to why God created us . . . there is no other reason except to bring glory to the Creator. We are created to have a relationship with God and to worship Him both in life and eternity. That's a pretty wild thought, I know. Most of us have trouble thinking about what we're having for dinner tonight, let alone comprehending eternity. We're just trying to survive the everyday challenges of motherhood. But let's think deeply for just a moment to grasp a firm understanding of this truth. You and I are created for the sole purpose of worshiping God. That puts a spin on how we use our minutes, doesn't it?

Many years ago I read a *Christianity Today* article entitled "Two Minutes to Eternity." A father who lost a child at birth and a special-needs daughter at the age of two wrote about his journey to understand the senselessness of their deaths. "Why would God create a child to live for two minutes?" he asked.[2] Eventually he came to understand that God doesn't create a child to live for two minutes, two years, or any number of years in a lifetime. God creates for eternity. Earth is our temporary home and heaven is our eternal home. Our worship on this earth is nothing compared to the worship we'll be able to give to God in eternity.

Living life God's way is the kind of worship God desires here on this earth. He wants our songs that we sing on Sunday, but

2. Marshall Shelley, *Christianity Today*, vol. 38, no. 6, May 16, 1994.

He wants us to live out those words every other day of the week. God says, "Anyone who sets himself up as 'religious' by talking a good game is self-deceived. This kind of religion is hot air and only hot air. Real religion . . . is this: Reach out to the homeless and loveless in their plight, and guard against corruption from the godless world"(James 1:26–27 msg). It seems logical that we could substitute the word *worship* for the word *religion* in this verse and better understand what God sees at the heart of things. In fact, that's what real worship is . . . a God-attitude of the heart.

What Did Jesus Do?

Jesus' life was an act of worship. He had a God-filter on everything that He did. He healed to give glory to God. He served others and gave God the credit. He loved unconditionally. He spoke truth. He extended compassion. He was filled with grace. He corrected with love and encouraged with truth. He was humble, gentle, and sacrificial.

Jesus had a God-filter on everything that He did.

I think what strikes me most, however, are the circumstances under which He did these things. He was in a world that was hostile to Him and the message He brought. He was highly criticized by those who didn't believe Him. And He was in high demand by those who did believe Him. There just didn't seem to be enough of Jesus to go around. Does that sound familiar in any way to your life as a mom? It sure does for me. Sometimes I feel stretched in so many different directions that I'm just sure I'm going to break! I'm sure Jesus felt that way at times. And I'm sure it was hard for Him to be in a hostile environment where He most likely was tempted to spend more time defending Himself than even bringing the message He came to bring.

But even in all of that, Jesus lived His life with godly character. Yes, I know, He *was* God so why would we expect anything different? We wouldn't necessarily expect anything different, but I believe the way Jesus lived His life strengthens us in two ways.

First, Jesus lived in a world that was hostile to Him and what He was trying to accomplish. At every turn He had someone questioning His identity and calling Him a liar. As mothers, we, too, live in a hostile environment today. It's an anti-family, anti-God world of moral relativism and decaying family values. Jesus knows what it feels like to be swimming upstream against a strong current! He lived it. His success laid the path for our success.

Second, we know that Jesus struggled with the reality of what God was asking Him to do. He knew He was sent to save a lost world, but He also knew that required His physical torture and then painful death. Even in the garden of Gethsemane, right before He was arrested and ultimately sent to the cross, He said, "My Father, if it is possible, may this cup be taken from me" (Matthew 26:39).

Although we can't compare what we're going through with the agony Jesus faced on the cross, every mom has experienced the feeling of "God, I don't think I can do this anymore." Our "cup" may be getting up for the sixth time in the night with a newborn or a sick child, or facing the challenges that come with a special-needs child or a hormonal teenager. Like Jesus, we often struggle with finding it within ourselves to continue with our assignment in life.

How Do I Worship As a Mom?

Being with kids day in and day out can mess with our perspective. Even if your kids are older, the demands of managing multiple schedules, teenage hormones, and learning to let go will throw you into a tailspin. It becomes so easy to see only the dirty diaper in front of our eyes and not see the bigger picture of how changing that diaper is an act of service which, done with a right perspective and attitude, is actually an act of worship.

Most of us have never thought of our everyday mothering responsibilities in such a spiritual way. But we need to, because Jesus led the way. God says, "Work with enthusiasm, as though you were working for the Lord rather than for people" (Ephesians 6:7 NLT). I love the wording that *The Message* translation uses: "And work with a smile on your face, always keeping in mind that no matter who happens to be giving the orders, you're really serving God." That's God's truth for us! Truth that gets us through hard nights. Truth that gives us a higher purpose for all the menial tasks we do each day. Truth that redefines our motives and changes our attitudes. Truth that will shape us, mold us, and transform us to be more like Jesus, if we'll allow it. Ultimately it is truth that frees us to be the wives and moms we long to be, defined by Jesus Christ, not by the trappings or expectations of the world we live in. And when we are able to understand that, we are able to worship God freely with our lives each and every day.

Many years ago, Karla Worley sang a song at one of our Hearts at Home conferences and the words have forever been etched in my mind:

> *My friend, Suzie, what a gal,*
>
> *Married twelve years to her childhood pal;*
>
> *Got a baby who's three now and one on the way . . .*
>
> *You can imagine how she spends her day.*
>
> *Down on her knees teachin' ABC's and bein' a faithful wife;*

Getting paid in kisses and pictures of fishes,

What a wonderful life!

And that's the way we praise Him: by the things we do and say;

Old men and children, young men and maidens, every day.

It's the single, simple secret that unlocks the universe:

That it's in the very ordinary puttin' Him first.

That's the way we praise Him.

We praise God—we worship Him—by putting Him first in our hearts and our minds. And when we do that, our attitude is the first thing to change.

Let God Transform Your Perspective

Sometimes I have to deal with my addictions. Oh, they're not the type of addictions you normally hear about like alcohol or drug addictions. But I'm addicted nonetheless. For instance, I'm addicted to control. I like my ducks in a row. I like things my way. And if I'm really honest with myself, I often think that my way is the only right way. One day God and I had a conversation about this. It went something like this:

God: *"Jill, that thing about control that you have—it's really about pride."*

Jill: "Pride . . . really? Pride is when someone is stuck on themselves. It's when they think they are better than others."

God: *"You think that your ideas are better than your husband's ideas sometimes."*

Jill: "Not always."

God: *"Jill . . . "*

Jill: "Okay, you're right. I guess I never thought about that as pride."

God: *"Sometimes we can't see things as they are and that's why we need truth in our life."*

Jill: "I'm sorry, Lord. Will You please forgive me?"

God: *"Absolutely. I forgive you."*

Lest you think that God was sitting in my living room having the conversation with me, it actually happened while I was on the way to pick up my boys from school. I was doing the argument thing in my head. You know, that's when you play out a whole argument with someone in your head. You say all the things you want to say that puts them in their place and brings you out on top. We've all done it. But somewhere in the middle of that, God's truth pricked my heart. I became convicted of my wrong attitude. He whispered gently, and I listened in that moment and the above conversation brought much-needed correction to me and a changed perspective.

Over the next few days God took that conversation a little further. He took me to Exodus 20 in the Bible where you can read the Ten Commandments. The first commandment is "You shall have no other gods before me" (verse 3). I've read that many times before, but this time it struck me differently. All of a sudden I saw pride differently. I had never thought about it this way before, but it is actually the worship of ourselves. We begin to think, often subconsciously, that our ways are the best ways—even better than

God's ways—so we move our eyes off God and onto ourselves. We worship the wrong thing.

But that's not the only thing we do that with. For instance, have you ever considered that worry is the worship of our circumstances? Or that unforgiveness or bitterness is the worship of a hurt caused by someone else? Our human nature too easily worships other gods. God knew this would happen and that's why He gave us His truth to get us back on the right road when our heart takes a detour.

So what's a mom to do when her heart gets off track? She moves her eyes from the mountains to the Mountain Mover! You and I need God-perspective every moment that we can get it. Because most of what we do in motherhood is serving others, it is so easy to get a skewed perspective that puts us in a bad mood and definitely affects the tone of our home. I've found three things that help me move my eyes to the Mountain Mover:

So what's a mom to do when her heart gets off track? She moves her eyes from the mountains to the Mountain Mover!

1. God's Truth: The Bible is full of wisdom, truth, and perspective for us. We need to keep it in front of us as much as possible. When my children were little, I got in the habit of putting a little Bible anywhere I might be sitting for a moment: in each bathroom, next to the rocking chair in the baby's room, next to the recliner in the family room where I nursed the baby, and next to my bed where I could read one little nugget before I fell asleep. As the kids grew older I added a Bible to my purse and in the glove compartment of my car so I could maximize time waiting during piano lessons, soccer practice, orthodontist appointments, and such. Now my Bible is on my smartphone and available to me all the time!

2. Holy Spirit: When we read the Bible, we increase the Holy Spirit's vocabulary in our lives. God gives us the Holy Spirit to guide us through daily life. When I felt the conviction about pride that I shared earlier, it was the nudge of the Holy Spirit on my heart that addressed my pride and spoke truth to me. I'd read about pride before, but the Holy Spirit took that knowledge from my head to my heart. When we let God's truth sink into our heart and ultimately change us, that's the purest form of worship we'll ever experience.

3. Faith Friends: We all need Christian friends who listen to our heart but aren't afraid to call a spade a spade. I have several friends that I can trust to be honest with me and speak truth when I need to hear it. Some of my best faith friendships were formed in my moms group as we took our friendships outside of the group and built nurturing and accountability relationships. While I'm no longer in a moms group, I find those relationships through church and other ministry opportunities I'm a part of. When I'm ready to throw in the towel with my challenging teenager, my friend MarLo will say, "Jill, God doesn't give us more than we can handle. You can do this." That's a paraphrase of Philippians 4:13 (NLT), "I can do everything through Christ who gives me strength."

Transformed Worship

Every mom faces the challenge of keeping a God-perspective in everything she does. However, when we are able to let God define us, mold us, and transform us we'll never see what we do every day as a mom in the same way. Because our heart—our attitude—is what God really wants, we have to be willing to let Him do a heart tune-up or even heart surgery when our spiritual health is diseased by sin. And when our heart is healthy, we're able to live a life of true worship.

When we do laundry with a right attitude, it's worship. When we prepare meals for our family with a right heart posture, it's worship. When we drive ten miles out of our way to take our husband his cell phone that he accidentally left at home and we do it with a heart of grace and forgiveness, it's worship.

Jesus lived a life of worship. His heart had a God-filter on it and He saw the world through God's eyes. May we, as moms, worship God with our hearts and our lives every day.

Lord, Give me Your eyes. Help me to see the world through Your perspective. Show me when I'm worshiping other gods in my life and help me to keep my eyes on You in everything that I do. Amen.

BRING CONTINOUSLY TO MY MIND, Holy Spirit, the truth that I can choose to worship You in absolutely every mundane thing. Please deal with my pride and control issues and help me to really see where I'm worshipping anything other than You.

Perspective

Can I please go to the bathroom alone?

J stumbled down the stairs in my early Monday-morning stupor. Mornings aren't my strong suit and it takes quite a bit of time for me to feel lucid. I closed the bathroom door for my first trip of the morning, only to hear my teenage daughter yell up the stairs, "Mom, did you wash my gym clothes?" Within seconds, I heard her slightly younger brother bellow, "Mom, if you are picking me up early today, I need a note." I'd barely been in the bathroom for a full minute before eight-year-old Erica was knocking on the door announcing that her two-year-old brother was awake and had produced a very dirty diaper sometime during the night.

I closed my eyes and thought, *Can't I just have two minutes alone in the bathroom?*

When Jesus walked on this earth, the Bible tells us that "large crowds followed him wherever he went" (Matthew 4:25 NLT). Whether you have one child or a whole houseful, the concept of being followed everywhere you go is one you have to get adjusted to when you become a mother. It begins right after birth or adoption. Suddenly you can no longer walk out the door without considering the needs of this new little one. A simple trip to the store requires a diaper bag full of baby supplies and a vast array of baby paraphernalia.

If you add more children to the family, the crowd becomes larger with time. And as children grow older, it's rare that they want to embark on any endeavor without a friend in tow. Let's face it—large crowds follow us everywhere we go!

Some moms relish this constant activity of kids and their friends, and some moms find themselves overwhelmed and stifled by it. I enjoy the constant activity but can only handle it for a limited time. Because of my people skills and ability to handle most social settings with ease, I've assumed that I was an extrovert. However, as I've become more in tune with myself, I've actually discovered I'm an introvert. I've also discovered that the terms "introvert" and "extrovert" don't really have much to do with your people skills. Instead they are really more about how you are emotionally drained and refueled. Simply put, being with people refuels an extrovert and being alone refuels an introvert.

So what does an introvert mother of five children do? She learns to take care of herself and get the alone time she desperately wants to find the emotional refueling she desperately needs. I've learned to find a bathroom in the middle of the day, or to seek the refuge of my front porch during the kids' nap or rest time. I've asked my husband to take the kids to the park occasionally so I can have time alone at home. I've learned to take an evening out once a week to go for a walk alone, or meet a friend for pie and coffee. This is not only beneficial for me, but for my family as well. When I'm running on a full emotional fuel tank, I'm more patient, more effective, and far more enjoyable to be around.

Conversely, what does an extrovert mother of one do? She learns to take care of herself by seeking out a moms group she can become a part of. She invites another mother and her children over for peanut butter and jelly sandwiches for lunch. She organizes a ladies night out for the moms in the neighborhood. And even though being with people refuels her, an extrovert mom still needs to find quiet moments to nourish her soul.

Jesus was intentional about finding time to refuel. He knew there were many demands upon His time and energy and He had to be a good steward of His body, soul, and mind. Nobody had to tell Him, "Jesus, go rest." Instead He recognized His need to pull away from the crowds and find the refreshment He needed.

As moms, we need to do the same. People and responsibilities demand much from us and we have to be good stewards of our body, soul, and mind. We can't wait until we're drained dry or until someone comes along and offers to watch our kids (like that happens very often!). Instead we have to learn to be proactive about our self-care so that we can be ready to meet the needs of our family.

Talk to God about the demands you feel upon you. Where do you feel smothered by them? What wears you down? Pour your heart out to Him about how you feel and where you feel pulled in a dozen different directions. After all, "large crowds followed him wherever he went." He really understands.

Pray . . .

Thank you, God, for having an understanding heart.
You didn't have much personal space in Your life and I often feel
I don't have much personal space in mine. Thank You for Your
example of intentionally refueling with rest and prayer, and intentionally
pulling away from the crowds. Help me learn to do the same

and to recognize the benefit for my family
and myself when I do so. In Jesus name, Amen.

Talk to God about the demands on your time and your desire to
learn how to be more intentional about self-care. Just talk to Him
like you would any friend—remember He's a Friend who understands.

Lord, what I need to be intentional about
is learning to rest with You and how to,
in my down time, focus on You instead
of all my tasks. Help my mind to learn
peace and self control and to learn to
rest in You and with You.

Discover …

Read Matthew chapters 5 and 6.

Ask God to help you see Jesus in a new light.

TRUTH …

Before daybreak the next morning, Jesus got up
and went out to an isolated place to pray.

MARK 1:35 (NLT)

12/31/16

CHAPTER 3

DISCOVER GOD'S TRUTH:
JESUS WAS COMPASSIONATE AND TENDER

The Truth about a Gentle Spirit

rica began to panic at the prospect of the immunization she was about to receive. The fear that set in caused her to "awfulize" the situation in her mind. She cried uncontrollably and was on the verge of hyperventilating. I wanted to take her face in my hands and tell her to "get a grip." My patience was wearing thin with my seventeen-year-old who I felt was acting like a two-year-old. Just as I was about to let my tongue go, a nurse walked in who had given Erica an immunization several months earlier. She knelt beside her and began to talk with her. She was tender, funny, and reassuring. Her kindness and humor brought a welcome distraction to the situation and within minutes Erica had calmed down.

Compassion and kindness had won out. A tender, gentle heart had conquered the fear. And I was convicted. Convicted of how often I jump to anger and don't even think about the tender, gentle way that I could approach the situation.

Our Example

Once we know God as our Savior, we begin a lifelong journey to make Him our Lord. The goal of that journey is to become more Christlike every day. There are several areas of my life in which I've been able to easily move aside while Christ takes over in the driver's seat. I've been able to die to my flesh without too much battle. But this particular trait of being compassionate and tender and having a gentle spirit will most likely be a lifelong expedition for me.

I'm a straight-shooting, tell-it-like-it-is person. I don't deal with feelings very often—in my mind they are not dependable. Give me the facts, please. I seek out and make decisions from knowledge, not emotion. I'm an analytical thinker rather than an emotional feeler.

I know there are a few women out there who are wired like I am. There's probably not too many of us, though. We'd find more men than women with those kinds of traits. But that's not a mistake God made. My personality makeup is what helps me to be the Hearts at Home leader God calls me to be. My personality makeup is exactly the opposite of my husband, who is more gentle and compassionate, and we balance each other out beautifully. My emotional wiring helps me to not take criticism personally, which is very important when living in the fishbowl that a ministry family lives in. But my personality doesn't serve me well when it comes to having a gentle spirit and feeling compassion or empathy for another person.

God doesn't want me to deny who He created me to be, but He wants to expand who I am to include more compassion, love, and mercy. It's so opposite to what comes naturally to me, and at times it seems impossible. But with God, nothing is impossible! (See Matthew 19:26.) When we become more like Christ we learn to live less in the flesh—our human ways—and more in the Spirit—like Christ's ways.

In the Bible there's a story known as "The Woman at the Well." This was a time when Jesus and the disciples were traveling from Judea to Galilee. Along the way, they had to go through Samaria. The background info you need for this story is that Jesus was a Jew and Jews did not associate with Samaritans. Not only that, but in Jesus' time, women did not have much value at all. Most men didn't bother to speak to a woman. But, of course, Jesus was different.

"Jesus, tired as he was from the journey, sat down by the well. . . . When a Samaritan woman came to draw water, Jesus said to her, 'Will you give me a drink?' . . . The Samaritan woman said to him, 'You are a Jew and I am a Samaritan woman. How can you ask me for a drink?'" (Read the story in John 4:4–30. The parts quoted are from the NIV.)

Jesus and the woman continued in conversation for quite some time about real water and living water. Real water quenches our thirst. Jesus used the real water that she had come to the well to draw as an analogy of the living water He offered that quenches our spiritual thirst. He was gentle, patient, and kind as He shared with her about this living water that really represented eternal life found only in a relationship with Christ.

After they converse about the water for a while Jesus then says something very interesting. "He told her, 'Go, call your husband and come back.' 'I have no husband,' she replied. Jesus said to her, 'You are right when you say you have no husband. The fact is, you have had five husbands, and the man you now have is not your husband. What you have just said is quite true.'"

Isn't that interesting? There are no secrets with Jesus—He knew this woman had been married five times and that the man she was currently living with wasn't even her husband. Yet He conversed with her in a way that allowed her to bring that to the surface. He didn't bring out the judge's gavel and say, "Girlfriend, you are messed up! What are you doing living with a man that you are not married to! Stop looking for love in all the wrong places!" Instead He was gentle and kind, drawing her out with His grace and mercy rather than condemning her with His judgment and anger.

Oh, how I need to learn to be more like Him! All too often I jump to conclusions and launch into judgments. I lecture when I should listen. I allow anger to cloud over patience and wisdom. And I handle things Jill's way instead of God's way.

A friend of mine shared how her teenage daughter had come home drunk one evening in her last year of high school. This was very much out of character for this child, so it caught the mom by surprise. She'd never dealt with this with her older children either. She sent an arrow prayer to God saying "Lord, show me what to do." My friend is wired like I am—a straight-shooting, call-it-like-it-is mom. Her normal manner of handling this would have been anger and she would have gone into lecture mode. But suddenly, in answer to her quick prayer, she had incredible compassion for her child. She found a peace overtake her that she couldn't explain as anything but God's presence and direction in her life. She sat on her daughter's bed and held her sweet girl while she cried and cried and cried. The conviction, the disappointment in herself, the reality of disappointing her parents all came crashing down as the tears flowed for what was probably close

It was a surreal hour; it was almost an out-of-body experience. But isn't that what Christlikeness is all about? We leave our human ways (the flesh) and pursue God's ways (the Spirit). When God is really in control we might not even recognize ourselves in the midst of letting Him lead.

to an hour. Her daughter sobbed, "I can't believe you're being this kind to me." Mom responded with, "Only with God's strength." Mom later communicated that it was a surreal hour; it was almost an out-of-body experience. But isn't that what Christlikeness is all about? We leave our human ways (the flesh) and pursue God's ways (the Spirit). When God is really in control we might not even recognize ourselves in the midst of letting Him lead.

That mom reported that in the months following this incident, the relationship between mother and daughter strengthened. A new trust grew between them. Had Mom operated in her flesh, a chasm would have certainly formed between the two of them. Because she operated in the Spirit, it brought the two of them together and formed a bond that was stronger than ever.

Remember When?

An important part of compassion is empathy. Empathy is identifying with or understanding another's situation, feelings, or motives. It's learning to walk in someone else's shoes.

Every mom was a teenager once in her life, but it's amazing how much we forget about the hormones and emotions we dealt with during those years. We all struggled with a friendship sometime during our childhood, but we're so far removed from that experience that we fail to remember the heartbreak we experienced. Sometimes we need to slow down and reminisce a little, tapping into the experiences and emotions we once felt. We need to stop trying to give answers and to give understanding instead. This is so hard for me! I'm a problem solver! But sometimes my husband, children, and girlfriends don't need their problems solved. They just need to know they're not alone. They need to know someone has walked through a similar experience and made it to the other side!

For the past ten years, my husband and I have shared publicly about our marriage struggles. We've talked about the heartache caused by pornography, the damage brought about by criticism, and the anguish carried into the marriage by premarital sex. Because we've been so open about our challenges, we've also had the opportunity to mentor hurting couples. One of the most powerful parts of that mentoring relationship is that they are talking to someone who understands. The empathy builds trust and the trust brings about honesty.

Sometimes I've asked myself why I can empathize so well in that setting, yet I struggle to do so with my children and husband. What I've come to realize is that it comes down to *time*. When Mark and I meet with a couple we are mentoring, we set aside two hours each week to sort through, listen to, and encourage the couple. I rarely give each member of my family that kind of focused attention. In fact, their crisis usually happens right about dinnertime when I feel like I have other responsibilities to attend to. Or they want to talk when I'm tucking them in bed and at that point, I'm counting down the minutes to being "off the clock" as a mom. You know what I mean . . . it's that moment when you can take a deep breath and say, "Whew! I made it. They're all in bed and I can have a few minutes to myself!" But then they want to talk and I'm running thin on patience.

What I've had to do is learn to see those moments not as interruptions, but rather God appointments. Those are moments I didn't plan for, but God did. We see Jesus doing this quite often. When He had His chat with the woman at the well, He wasn't stopping in Samaria to see her. He and the disciples made a pit stop—kind of like stopping at a rest area along the interstate. But God had an appointment there. We don't see Jesus saying, "Man, can I get away from this ministry stuff? I just want to get a drink, take a break, and rest My body before traveling some more." Instead, He captures the opportunity right there in front of Him. Ministry for Jesus was the person standing in front of Him. And ministry for you and me is the person standing in front of us: our husband, our child, our friend, our neighbor.

Reality Check

Before we go any further, I think it's very important to remember that while we are getting to know Jesus as our Friend and learning to live life His way, we will still mess up along the way. Not one of us will get it right every time. We'll lose our patience, gentleness will go right out the window, and our anger will overtake any sense of compassion in us. We'll choose harsh words that come out quickly over tender words that take time to formulate in my mind. Bottom line, we'll all give our children a reason to sit across from Dr. Phil someday!

Because we're human, we will mess up. But because we have a Savior, God has given us a way to clean up our messes. The Bible tells us in 1 John 1:9, "If we confess our sins, he is faithful and just and will forgive us." It's exactly the same process we tell our kids to take when they make a mistake. You say "I'm sorry. Will you please forgive me?" In this case, however, we're not saying that to another person, we're saying it to God. And do you know what His answer is? It's always, "Yes!" It's absolutely, always yes. If we truly have a repentant heart (we're sorry for what we did, not just sorry we got caught), He forgives and wipes the slate clean. "The Lord is full of compassion and mercy" (James 5:11). We experience His compassion and mercy first and then we're able to pass it on to others.

So when you and I mess up (and we will mess up), we have to do business with God first. This is how we keep our hearts cleaned up and sensitive to God's leading. If we don't take care of business, our heart becomes hard, bitter, and numb to feel God's presence in our life. To be more like Christ, we have to have a soft, open spirit to God and His truth. So taking care of our own heart business with God is vital to becoming more compassionate and more like Christ.

Some of us struggle with acknowledging our sins, weaknesses, or failures. We too easily play the blame game or too quickly try to minimize the mistake. Pride gets in the way and keeps us hardened to God and His truth. Through owning our own stuff and confession to God, we are pursuing internal renovations that build our character, repaint our perspective, and reorganize our thoughts to be God-focused instead of me-focused. That's a makeover job that's always in process when a person wants to be more like Christ.

Once we've done business with God, we may or may not need to do business with others. Let me give you an example for both situations. There are seasons of my life when I move along and kind of forget to talk with God. Life's going along just fine and as long as there's no crisis, I unconsciously move God from the front burner to the back burner. "What's wrong with that?" you might ask. In reality many of us go day after day without praying. Is that really a sin? Well, it's the sin of pride because pride says, "I can do it on my own, thank you very much. I don't need Your help, God." Once I realize that's what's going on in my heart and mind, I need to take care of business with God. He's the only one who's been directly affected by my sin. I talk to Him humbly and say, "God, I'm so sorry that I've been prideful in my heart. I don't want that—I really do want humility and I want to trust You more than I trust me. That's so hard to do, but I know it's not impossible. I'm sorry for my pride. Will You please forgive me?"

But let's say that in the midst of that prayerless week or two, I'm very irritable with my kids or very critical of my husband. We are who we hang with and if we're not hanging around Jesus and spending time with Him, it will often be evident in our interactions with others. In this case I begin by doing business with God, admitting my pride and prayerlessness and asking for forgiveness. Then I do business with my family, apologizing for my impatience, irritability, and criticism, and asking for their forgiveness.

By allowing God to mop up our messes with His forgiveness, we become more humble, gentle, and forgiving ourselves. When we realize that we're no different from anyone else around us—we all mess up—then we become more tender and empathetic because it puts us all on level playing ground. You and I can't become compassionate like Christ without identifying our own imperfections.

> When we realize that we're no different from anyone else around us—we all mess up—then we become more tender and empathetic because it puts us all on level playing ground.

Mommy Matters

It was a day that felt like everyone needed me. Mark needed my help with a church event. Anne had called two or three times. Evan had done the same (both Anne and Evan are grown and out of the home). Erica was in her final few weeks of the spring semester of homeschooling. Austin and Kolya both had homework they needed help with. I had stayed up late several nights in a row and the lack of sleep was affecting me more than I cared to admit. I'd had my time with Jesus each morning, but somewhere around 5:00 p.m. on that Wednesday night I lost it. I don't remember which kid asked for what thing but it didn't matter because I fell apart at the twenty-fifth request for help that came my way and the mommy mentor turned into the mommy monster. Talk about having to go back and clean up a mess!

Even though I did the right spiritual things to bring about the gentle, tender spirit I longed to have with my kids, I didn't have the emotional and physical stamina to sustain the patience needed for gentleness to reign. Bottom line, I was too tired and didn't have the energy that gentleness required. And believe me . . . gentleness, tenderness, and compassion take a lot of physical and emotional energy! Being quiet and patient takes a lot more energy than losing it and screaming. It seems like it would be the other way around, but self-control takes energy.

What I'm getting at is the fact that the art of self-care plays into our ability to be gentle, tender, and compassionate. We need to keep our physical fuel tank filled up with good rest whether by a full night's sleep or naps during the day. If you have an infant you are probably wondering how in the world you can make that happen. And if you have an infant and a toddler or two you're probably wondering if I've fallen off the deep end. But I've been there before myself. With five children spanning thirteen years, I had an infant or a preschooler in our home for seventeen straight years. What I learned in those years was to nap when the baby napped and to require my preschoolers to take a minimum of a one-hour rest time each day. They thought it was for them . . . but really it was for me! I also learned to force my body into the bed for what seemed like an unnaturally early bedtime at times. This was the proactive way to get the rest I needed rather than depend on occasional naps to make up for my late nights.

We also need to keep our emotional fuel tank filled up by crafting "mommy moments" into our crazy days. A mommy moment might be putting your feet up and reading a book while the kids have a rest time (and yes, that means you'll have to let the dishes go or wait to fold a load of laundry until a little later!). A mommy moment might be a night out with the girlfriends or attending a moms group that offers a quality program for you and quality child care for your children. And a mommy moment might be chatting a few minutes on the phone or online with a girlfriend who understands.

Sometimes you have to ask for help to find a mommy moment. I occasionally asked a friend to keep my kids so I could take some time to myself or catch up on my sleep. I asked my husband for one evening a week that was "Daddy Night" for the kids. They knew they would have Dad all to themselves and I knew I could depend on one night to myself each week. I traded "days off" with another mom so every other week we each had a Mommy Moment Day of our own. Mommy moments are not selfish—they are self-sustaining and an important part of taking care of ourselves so we can take care of our family with a compassionate and gentle spirit.

I Want to Be Like You!

"Mom, I'm scared," said the preschool boy who didn't want his mom to leave his bedroom after she tucked him in. "Don't be scared," Mom reassured, "you're not alone. Jesus is with you." "I know that Jesus is with me," he replied, "but tonight I just need someone with skin on!"

I know it's a bit overwhelming to think about, but for our children, we're Jesus with skin on. Before they can understand who Jesus is, they have the opportunity to experience His character through us. Of course, we can't be perfect like Jesus is—we're not

God! But we can show our kids how to handle our human failures under the wings of God's forgiveness and grace.

There's nothing more powerful than to have a child aspire to be like their mom or dad. And that's especially inspiring when their parent aspires to be like Jesus. Jesus was tender, compassionate, and gentle in His interactions with other people. May we aspire to be more like Him.

God, I do want to be more like You, but I seem to be stuck in my ways so much of the time. Help me to be intentional about taking care of myself so I have the emotional and physical energy for a gentle, tender spirit. I want to learn to ask questions rather than give judgment or demand answers. Help me to put myself in other people's shoes. Remind me of how difficult fourth grade was for me so I can be more sensitive to my son. Take me back to high school to remember the challenges of peer pressure so I can relate better with my daughter. Help me to think about the environment my husband has been in all day before I lash out in anger because he forgot about something I asked him to do. Thank You for being my example and my Friend who understands.

Perspective

I'm in high demand.

"Mom, will you play ball with me? I need to work on my catching." "Mom, can you wash my cross-country shirt? I have a meet tonight." "Mom, can we go shopping today for a new pair of jeans? I've outgrown all the ones in my closet." "Mom, I need you to help me look through my catalog for classes for the fall semester. I have to register online by tomorrow." "Mom, can you pick up the silk flowers for my bridesmaids' bouquets today?"

Believe it or not, every one of those questions was posed to me by each of my five children, ages ten to twenty-one, within a thirty-minute period one summer day. By the time question number five was tossed my way, I wanted to scream, "There's not enough of me to go around!" Okay, I'll be honest. It wasn't one of my holier moments. I believe I did scream those words and a few more. Then I sent myself to my room, calmed down, apologized to my children, and asked for their forgiveness. And life continued on.[3]

Sometimes it honestly feels like there's not enough of me to go around. In my weaker moments, I'd like to say, "Mom's not

3. Jill Savage, *I'm Glad I'm A Mom* (Eugene, Ore.: Harvest House Publishers, 2007), 35.

here. She left the building and cannot be found." But the truth is I am in great demand. Whether it's helping my child find a lost tennis shoe in the bedroom or helping my husband find the ketchup bottle right in front of him in the refrigerator, Mom's the one with the answer.

This isn't an unfamiliar experience for Jesus. He, too, was in high demand. *Jesus, will You come heal my daughter? Jesus, will You turn the water into wine? Jesus, will You calm the storm? Jesus . . . Jesus . . . Jesus!*

In my home, and I'm sure in your home, it's *Mommy . . . Mom . . . Mommmmmmmmy!* People are always calling us or needing something from us. When Jesus lived on this earth, people were always calling Him and needing something from Him. Once when Jesus had gone out to pray, some of the disciples went out to find Him. "When they found him they said, 'Everyone is looking for you' (Mark 1:37 NLT). Can you relate to that? I can! Jesus was tugged in many different directions, and that's a challenge you and I experience many times as a mom.

Looking at Jesus' life, however, I've come to understand that while there were many people who needed Him, He didn't meet all of the needs around Him. There were many who called His name that He was not able to or chose not to answer. In His human form, there simply wasn't enough of Him to go around at times; and, as we've already noted, He had to also know His physical limits. The Bible tells us, "Jesus instructed his disciples to have a boat ready so the crowd would not crush him. He had healed many people that day, so all the sick people eagerly pushed forward to touch him" (Mark 3:9–10 NLT). There were so many people and He could not possibly meet all their needs. At some point He had to call it a night, pull away from the crowds, and be okay with some unmet needs.

You and I can't meet all the needs around us either. We have to know our limitations. We have to say no at times. Some of us have to let go of our perfectionist tendencies and go to bed with dirty dishes sitting on the counter or laundry left unfolded. If Jesus didn't meet all the needs around Him, why do I think I need to be able to meet all the needs around me? I'm beginning to understand how unrealistic that is.

Think about that for a few minutes. Talk with God about it. And while you're at it, cut yourself some slack. Our Friend Jesus understands the demands we face. But He also understands that we can't always meet every need around us.

Pray . . .

*Jesus, Thank You for Your ability to empathize with
our experience of being in high demand. Sometimes I feel
outnumbered and sometimes I feel numbed out. Help me to
know my limitations and live within them. Show me how to
spend time with You in such a way that it gives me
the energy needed for the demanding job of motherhood.*

*Take a few moments to talk with God (verbally or in written form)
about all of the people that need you, and your thoughts and
feelings about meeting those needs.*

_____

_____

_____

_____

Discover . . .

Read Matthew chapters 7, 8, and 9.
Use a highlighter to mark anything that seems to
jump out to you personally.

TRUTH . . .

I can do all things through Christ
who strengthens me.

PHILIPPIANS 4:13 (NKJV)

CHAPTER 4

DISCOVER GOD'S TRUTH:
JESUS WAS ANGRY

The Truth about Boundaries

J was supposed to bring dinner to a new mother at the church. On the day the meal was to be delivered, Austin came down with a fever. I left him at home with his homeschooled sister while I attended a parent-teacher conference for our son Kolya, who as an ESL (English as a Second Language) student had been struggling in school. After the conference, I dropped off a couple of boxes at the Hearts at Home office to be mailed. On the way home, I stopped by the store to pick up a few things we needed, remembering then that Mark needed food prepared for a meeting he was hosting the next day. I made my purchases and headed home. Once home, Erica needed some help with her schoolwork and Austin just wanted Mom to sit on the couch with him, rub his back, and watch a movie. When Mark came home, I was quite proud that I actually had dinner in the oven, considering the craziness of the day. When we sat down to eat, Mark's words stopped me in my tracks, "Jill, this is a great meal. Is this what you took to Amanda's family tonight too?" I choked on the food I had just put in my mouth as I gasped in horror. In the midst of everything that had happened, I had completely forgotten to take the meal to the new mom! I was horrified as I pictured them sitting there waiting for me to bring their dinner, which should have been delivered well over an hour ago. I rushed to the phone and dialed Amanda, apologizing all over the place and offering to order them a pizza that would be delivered to their home. This sweet young mom was so gracious and reassured me that they had so many leftovers from the other meals brought that they had already warmed up some food and eaten. I felt like such a failure. How could I forget something I'd promised to do for someone else? When I evaluated that incident over the next few days, I came to realize that it had nothing to do with that particular day, but it had everything to do with how much was on my plate in general. I had enough going on that week that I had no business saying yes to bringing a meal. I needed to set some boundaries, and then I needed to abide by them.

Drawing the line

When the Passover Feast, celebrated each spring by the Jews, was about to take place, Jesus traveled up to Jerusalem. He found the Temple teeming with people selling cattle and sheep and doves. The loan sharks were also there in full strength.

Jesus put together a whip out of strips of leather and chased them out of the Temple, stampeding the sheep and cattle, upending the tables of the loan sharks, spilling coins left and right. He told the dove merchants, "Get your things out of here! Stop turning my Father's house into a shopping mall!" That's when his disciples remembered the Scripture, "Zeal for your house consumes me." (John 2:13–17 MSG)

This is one time we really see Jesus angry in the Bible. He was very upset about the way this place of worship was being used. It wasn't honoring to God and it abused what was considered sacred. In His actions to clear the temple, Jesus was putting a boundary in place. He was drawing a line. It was driven by purpose and passion—both which are needed to draw healthy boundary lines in our lives, as well.

Jesus' purpose was to bring salvation to a lost world. He became the living sacrifice to ultimately connect a lost world to the God who created them. Knowing that His job was to die on the cross so we could live brought about a purpose that was clear and a passion for truth. Everything He did, He did through His filter of passion and purpose. And once again, He modeled for us how to live life on this earth.

But I'm Just a Mom . . .
What's My Passion and Purpose?

Jesus knew what His job was here on this earth. The vision and energy with which He pursued that purpose made up His passion. He walked out every day of His life with that understanding.

You and I desperately need to know what our purpose is and we need to pursue it with passionate energy and vision. But most of us have no sense of purpose in our daily responsibilities as moms and we find it hard to be passionate about doing the same tasks over and over again each day. This is the challenge of motherhood that each of us faces.

When I first became a mom, I was in the midst of pursuing my college degree. Married the summer after my freshman year of college, I found out I was expecting just eleven months later. Anne was due to arrive during the second semester of my junior year.

Since she was due in February, I took off the spring semester to have her and headed right back to school in the fall. I had my eyes set on my degree and nothing . . . not even motherhood . . . was going to get in my way. By the first semester of my senior year, I found myself expecting again and Evan arrived on the day of my college graduation ceremonies. Needless to say, I didn't participate in commencement but received my much-awaited diploma in the mail. I knew what my purpose was—I'd been working toward it for four and a half years! I was made to be a music teacher and I could see myself doing nothing else.

After a move from Indiana to Illinois to allow my husband to pursue full-time ministry, I found myself in a predicament. I was made to teach music, but there were no teaching jobs in my specialty anywhere within a thirty-mile radius of our new home in Illinois. "But God . . . what am I going to do? I've worked for the past five years to ready myself to teach, and now there are no jobs. Mark is in school full-time and I need to bring in the income for us to live on. What do you want me to do?"

I lamented these things to God over the period of several months. In time, He showed me His plan for that season—I was to create a home day care and a private music studio in my home. Both would bring in an income and didn't require me to have to find day care for my children. In my mind, this was Plan B. What I soon came to realize is that in God's mind, it was Plan A. I've heard it said that

I've heard it said that if you want to hear God laugh, tell Him your plans.

if you want to hear God laugh, tell Him your plans. I'm thinking that during this season, I must have had Him rolling on the floor laughing so hard He had to be crying.

After a year of caring not only for my children, but also a half-dozen other children, I began to have a glimpse of the value of being home . . . at least for a season of time. After much discussion and prayer, Mark and I decided that I would be home until the kids were in school. That was a great plan, except that we kept having kids! Each time a preschooler was getting ready to go to school, the stick would turn blue! I ended up having a preschooler in the home for seventeen straight years! At that rate, it felt like I was going to be home for the rest of my life!

Somewhere along the way, however, I began to see mothering differently. I stopped looking at it from the perspective of a temporary season where I was waiting to pursue my "real" profession of teaching and I began looking at it as my profession. I took my mothering and homemaking responsibilities more seriously, set goals for my children and myself and became a much more intentional wife and mom. I stopped looking for a short-term sense of accomplishment and put my eye on one very long-term goal: to raise responsible, respectful, loving adults. My purpose became clear and my passion for the profession of motherhood grew.

Like Jesus, because I understood my purpose, it became easier to set boundaries. When a friend offered me a part-time job, I communicated that I didn't need another job—I had one already. When our fourth child was born, I gave up teaching private voice and piano lessons. My passion for the profession of motherhood was now stronger than my desire to teach. I had a vision and energy for motherhood that became a filter through which I made all decisions.

4. Henry Cloud and John Townsend, *Boundaries* (Grand Rapids: Zondervan, 1992), 25.

Boundaries Are Healthy

Most of us have trouble drawing lines in our life. Our desire to please others overshadows our ability to be true to ourselves. Drawing lines is actually a healthy thing to do. Dr. Henry Cloud and Dr. John Townsend state in their bestselling book *Boundaries* that "it takes wisdom to know what we should be doing and what we shouldn't. We can't do everything."[4]

Jesus knew that and lived out the principle of boundaries. He dismissed the crowd and then spent time with His Father (Matthew 14:22–23). He told the rich young ruler that He couldn't help him until he gave away the money that controlled him (Matthew 19:16–21). He refused to perform miracles just because King Herod hoped He would (Luke 23:8–9). He also said that we are to love God and love our neighbor as ourselves (Matthew 22:37–40). One way we learn to love ourselves is by setting boundaries.

Because I know my purpose as a mom is to raise morally responsible, respectful, loving adults, I can allow my children to experience the natural consequences of their poor choices. I don't carry the responsibility for those choices; I let them carry the responsibility themselves. That's a healthy boundary.

Because I know my purpose as a homemaker is to focus on my home and family, I don't carry false guilt when I need to say no to a request for volunteer time when all my volunteer hours are already full. That's a healthy boundary.

Because I know my purpose as a follower of Christ, I don't need to apologize when I stand firm in my faith and beliefs. That's a healthy boundary.

Because I know my purpose as a wife is to invest in my marriage, and love and respect my husband, I don't feel guilty when I have to say no to a moms group that wants me to speak on a Friday morning. Fridays are our date day for our marriage. That's a healthy boundary.

Saying no is as important as saying yes. Too many yeses and not enough noes results in an out-of-balance life.

Learn to Say No

Jesus said no when His mother and brothers tried to use their relationship to pull Him away from the people He was ministering to (Matthew 12:46–50). Jesus said no to Peter and the disciples who thought Jesus should be a political king or military warrior rather than a Savior who would go to the cross for us (Matthew 16:23). He said no to King Herod when he requested a miracle just for the purpose of entertainment (Luke 23:8–9). Following His example, we know it's perfectly okay for us to learn to say no as well.

In my book *Professionalizing Motherhood*, I share several suggestions for learning to say no. Understanding these strategies will help us follow Jesus' example.

1. Keep in mind that you know what is best for you and your family. With many mothers working outside the home, there are fewer school, church, and community volunteers available during the day. Therefore, an at-home mom is likely to be asked more often, simply because she is perceived to be more available. Remember, even with church activities, that our families are our first ministries.

2. Never say yes on the spot. Always tell them you will call them back after you've had time to pray and think about it. This keeps you from making an on-the-spot decision you may regret later. You can say no immediately if you know that the position or responsibility is wrong for you.

3. When considering a time commitment, make sure you take into account preparation time. Most of us underestimate the time it really takes to do a job. If you have been asked to bake five dozen cookies, look at the calendar and determine whether you truly have that much free time available before the cookies need to be delivered. If it looks too busy, say you're sorry, but you can't do it.

4. When considering long-term commitments, **make sure you consider all your household responsibilities** and the time constraints that accompany them. It may seem that becoming the president of an organization you really believe in will not take too much time. But after a few months, the phone calls, meetings, and errands have begun to take up the time you previously used for laundry, housecleaning, or paying the bills. These are big jobs that need to be integrated into your weekly and daily responsibilities. Don't allow your family responsibilities to be sacrificed for your volunteer responsibilities.

5. Carefully consider the "brain space" this responsibility will require. Have you ever been listening to your children, but really thinking about a new project or the hundreds of things you need to do? When your mind is cluttered, you are not mentally available to your family.

6. Remember every minute of your day does not have to be scheduled! If you have a doer mentality, you will think of a spare hour or two as a way to fit in one more yes. Yet we need some time to do nothing. If you need to, schedule in downtime each day. Write it on your calendar and say no to anything that would fill that time.

7. Set a limit to the number of long-term commitments you will carry. For instance, within the Hearts at Home organization we encourage women to carry no more than one large and one small long-term volunteer commitment. If they were to take on another long-term commitment, we would encourage them to give up one of their previous commitments. Limiting your long-term commitments allows for more time to help out in short-term service projects. You will be more likely to have the time to bake brownies for your child's classroom or be a teacher's assistant during vacation Bible school if you take a similar approach.

8. Ask for accountability. Ask your husband, a close friend, or your Bible study group to hold you accountable for the number of commitments you will carry. Be open to their insight. If you have trouble saying no, ask them to help you during the first few months while you get things back in balance. When you tell someone you will call them back, check with your accountability partner first before answering. Sort through your schedule with them. Eventually you won't need the partner's help, but it can help you while you are learning to say no.

9. When you do say no, don't feel that you need to give a long list of excuses. You know what is best for your family and for yourself. If you feel you need to give an excuse, simply say that it would not fit into your schedule at this time.

10. Keep in mind that you do not have to say yes simply because you are capable. You may have strong leadership skills and will most likely to be asked to lead most anything you will be involved in. That doesn't mean you have to say yes to those

responsibilities. You should say yes only after considering your time availability, other volunteer responsibilities, your family commitments, and what you might need to give up to properly do this job. Of course, above all, you should say yes only after praying and seeking God's will.

11. If you have too much on your plate now, reevaluate your priorities. Determine what responsibilities you need to let go of. Give a one-month notice to those organizations that you will no longer be able to serve. Although it may be difficult to give up a responsibility, you are not doing the organization or your family any good when you cannot fully commit to the job. As soon as you let go of some of the responsibilities you were carrying, instill new boundaries for your time. Don't let yourself become overcommitted again.

12. Remember that saying no allows others the opportunity to say yes. Don't take service opportunities away from others. Don't forget to make time to have a friend over, take your kids to the park, write a letter, or go on a date with your husband. We don't usually schedule these kinds of activities, but they are the first to go when we are overcommitted.

Remember that saying yes to some activities outside the home will be important to your sanity. Moms of young children need to get out of the house to socialize and think about something other than diapers, bottles, and coupons. Contrary to popular belief, your brain will not turn to mush—it will just feel like it at times. We need to carefully choose those activities we will be involved in so that our time will be used wisely. You will be amazed at the patience you will have with your family when you find balance in your activity schedule.[5]

5. Jill Savage, *Professionalizing Motherhood* (Grand Rapids: Zondervan, 2002), 55–58.

Is Anger Okay?

While the best-known example of Jesus' anger was His clearing the temple of those selling for profit, there may well have been other times He experienced anger, a godly, just anger. In Mark 3:5 (NLT) we read that "He looked around at them angrily and was deeply saddened by their hard hearts." We only see a few examples of Jesus being angry, but there are other times where He did get exasperated or frustrated with others—specifically the disciples (see Matthew 15:16)!

Jesus was just as human as you and me. Anger is a normal human emotion, and Jesus experienced that feeling just as we do. The only difference between our anger and His anger is that He didn't sin in His anger. Sometimes you and I do sin in our anger. Anger is a God-given emotion, while sinning in our anger refers to how we act in that emotion. It is possible to be angry and not sin. It takes a lot of self-control . . . but it's not impossible!

Anger is a normal human emotion, and Jesus experienced that feeling just as we do. The only difference between our anger and His anger is that He didn't sin in His anger.

Jesus' anger when He cleared the temple was a righteous anger, and righteous anger is an effective way to determine boundaries. There are actually times when we *should* be angry. Right anger takes a stand against injustice. It actually takes a stand with God because if something makes God angry it should make us angry. Injustice and immorality should make us mad—mad enough to do something about it and to stand firm on God's truth.

Love Fences

So many of us have an unbalanced picture of God. We only see the soft side of love and struggle with the balance of the hard side of love. Even in learning to love ourselves, there is a soft side of love where we practice the art of self-care, but there is a balance of the hard side of love where we learn to recognize that setting boundaries is actually a very loving action.

Jesus' anger in clearing the temple came out of His love for His Father. He cared enough to draw a line and say, "This isn't okay." When Jesus sent the crowds away so He could spend time with the Father, it was an act of love for the Father and for Himself. He also loved the people, but He knew He couldn't give to them out of His emptiness. He needed to spend time with the Father to be able to minister with a full spiritual and emotional tank.

As moms, sometimes the most loving thing we can do for our child is to tell them no. Many of us use a playpen or a safety gate with our toddlers. These wonderful inventions could actually be called "love fences." A mom who uses a "love fence" is saying no to letting the child go wherever he wants and possibly endanger or hurt himself. A mom who says no to her sixth-grade daughter who wants to go out on a date with a high-school boy is loving that child with a boundary. Parents who establish a curfew for a high-school son or daughter are saying no to being out all night because they love their child. Boundaries are love . . . established because we love God, love ourselves, and love others.

God, Help me to see boundaries as a good thing for my life. Too often I'm hesitant to draw lines in my life. I want others to like me and I'm afraid they won't like me if I say no. Help me to be a God-pleaser and not a people-pleaser. Thank You for the example of Your Son . . . may I grow to be more like Him every day.

1/29/17

Is there such a thing as uninterrupted sleep?

It was a Friday evening. Our boys were in bed and our two girls were away from home. Erica, who was in junior high, was spending the night at a friend's home. This was a rare experience for her as she had often called midway through the night on other such occasions asking to come home. Our daughter Anne was a freshman in college five hours from our home. I had spoken to her earlier in the evening after she'd had an enjoyable dinner out with her friends.

The phone rang shortly after midnight. Mark and I had been asleep around an hour. I deliriously grabbed the phone and heard the teary voice on the other end of the line, "Mom, I want to come home," she said through her sobs. Mark had already stumbled out of bed and was pulling on his jeans and tennis shoes. "Okay, Erica, Dad will be there to get you in just a few minutes." "Mom!" she replied. "This isn't Erica! This is Anne. Dad can't come to get me, I'm five hours away!"

I thought once my kids were out of the infant and toddler years, a full night's sleep was just around the corner. I've come to understand that it's probably not realistic to expect it until the nest is empty! Even in the teen years, I'm waiting up to make sure my child is home by curfew or I'm answering an unexpected phone call from my college student who's still going strong at midnight studying for a test. During the grade school and preschool years I was often up with a sick child or someone who had a bad dream. With three children with asthma, I've certainly done my fair share of 3:00 a.m. nebulizer treatments. Of course when there's a baby in the home who has to eat every three hours—uninterrupted sleep becomes a distant memory from the past.

Do you long for just one night of uninterrupted sleep? I'm sure there were times that Jesus felt that, too. One night He and His disciples were crossing a body of water after a long day of teaching. "A huge storm came up. Waves poured into the boat, threatening to sink it. And Jesus was in the stern, head on a pillow, sleeping! They roused him, saying, 'Teacher, is it nothing to you that we're going down?'" (Mark 4:37–38 MSG). I love that picture! The description wasn't just that Jesus was sleeping, but His head was on a pillow! And what did the disciples do? They woke Him up! What do our kids do when our head is on a pillow? They wake us up!

Maybe, like me, you had never thought about the fact that Jesus knows what it feels like to work hard all day and long to lay your head on a pillow for a good night's sleep, only to be awakened abruptly. Take a few minutes to ponder what a day and a night in Jesus' life might have looked like. Talk to God about things that go bump in the night. And marvel at the fact that even when it comes down to pillow talk, Jesus is a Friend who understands.

*Jesus, Thank You for the tiniest details that are included
in the biography books of the Bible. You laid Your head on a pillow!
You were tired, but even in the middle of the night You had to sacrifice
Your needs! You know how I feel. Thank You for understanding
my life, down to the smallest details.*

Your plate was so much fuller than mine and Your days more taxing. Your tasks more urgent. You understand physical weariness so very well. Thank You for understanding every physical aspect of my life, Jesus!

Discover . . .

*Read Matthew chapters 10 and 11.
Much of these chapters are Jesus' own words. As you read,
personalize what Jesus is saying specifically to you.*

TRUTH . . .

Come to me, all you who are weary
and burdened, and I will give you rest.

MATTHEW 11:28

CHAPTER 5

DISCOVER GOD'S TRUTH:
JESUS SACRIFICED

The Truth about Sacrifice

J just can't believe your skin can stretch like that!" my husband declared one day when I was in my ninth month of pregnancy. Honestly, I couldn't believe it either. I was long past being able to see my feet, my ankles were swollen, and I was definitely feeling like a beached whale. This was my fourth pregnancy . . . you would have thought we'd seen it all, but the reality of what new life does to an old body was still a miracle (or travesty!) to behold. I couldn't sleep comfortably, suffered from terrible indigestion, and was absolutely miserable, but just a few days later, we were holding our new bundle of joy. The sacrifice was worth it all.

Six years later, Mark and I sat in a run-down courtroom before a Russian judge. After months of paperwork, expense, and un-imaginable hours of time, we were on the verge of adding another son to our family, this time through adoption. We knew that Kolya belonged in our family; we now had to convince the judge of this.

The judge just couldn't understand why we would want a nine-year-old child from Russia when we had four of our own back in the United States. After many hours of answering questions with the help of a translator, the judge finally agreed to sign the papers. The sacrifice of thousands of dollars and hours finally paid off. Aaron Nikolai became a Savage.

Sacrificial Reality

Motherhood and sacrifice . . . the two words are synonymous. Whether you arrived at motherhood biologically or by adoption, you find out very soon that sacrifice is a part of the job. For most of us the sacrifice begins with pregnancy or those first steps toward adoption, but for moms who deal with infertility, sacrifice begins months, even years earlier.

I find it interesting that the root word of sacrifice is *sacred*—a word that means worthy of respect or regarded with reverence. Another meaning of sacred is something that is made or declared holy or something associated with divinity. Understanding that leads us right to our example of sacrifice: Jesus Christ.

To understand Jesus' life and ultimate sacrifice, we have to go back to the beginning . . . the beginning of time. On page one of the Bible, in the book of Genesis, we begin with God creating heaven and earth, water and dry land, light and darkness, and eventually man and woman. Man and woman lived in this perfect place called the garden of Eden. It was a place where they had a perfect relationship with God and each another, and where all their physical needs were met.

God gave Adam and Eve free will. In other words, He created them to live by His design and according to His ways but He allowed them to make those choices on their own. God gave them full access to the garden, putting only one boundary on them: they could not eat from one tree: the Tree of the Knowledge of Good and Evil. God's boundaries are always given to protect us. Even in this case, God was protecting Adam and Eve from having knowledge that would complicate their lives and introduce them to the concept of death.

One day in the garden, Satan tempted Adam and Eve to eat from the forbidden tree and they fell for his lies hook, line, and sinker. When they ate the fruit their eyes were opened and they suddenly saw life differently. They saw their nakedness and made themselves some clothes. Then, in shame, they hid from God. The garden, which had been a place of joy and fellowship, was now a place of fear and hiding from God. As a consequence of their disobedience, God required them to leave the garden of Eden. Because of that, life became harder—and now the fellowship with a holy God had been broken. You can read the story in Genesis chapters 1–3.

The entire Old Testament of the Bible tells the story of man's existence from creation until Jesus Christ was born. During this time, the only way that sinful people could have a relationship with a holy God was through sacrifice and a high priest who would stand in the gap between the people and God. The Israelites understood that God could have chosen to be a judge with no grace and mercy when Adam and Eve disobeyed. But instead of giving up on them, He chose to give them a second chance! This second chance was an opportunity for man and woman to be reconciled or reconnected to their Creator. But coming into the presence of God required an admission of sin (disobedience), and because a Holy God can't exist in the presence of sin, a sacrifice was offered to "cover" the sin. Most of the sacrifices offered in the Old Testament were lambs and they had to be offered through a priest who represented the people. The shedding of the blood covered the sins of the people so they could have relationship with a holy God.

But for God, this was a temporary plan. His decision to send His Son to earth was His ultimate plan for reconnecting to His people. Jesus came to this earth as fully God, yet fully man. One way God connected to us was by becoming one of us. We have a God who truly understands our human experience. But God's plan was more than simply understanding our human experience. He sent His Son to be the ultimate sacrifice and our High Priest. The Bible says, "We have a Priest-Friend in the presence of the Father: Jesus Christ, righteous Jesus. When he served as a sacrifice for our sins, he solved the sin problem for good—not only ours, but the whole world's" (1 John 2:2 MSG). Jesus came to share truth and eventually die on the cross as the final sacrifice for our sin. He died; then three days later He rose again and eventually went to live in heaven where He is the only priest needed—He's our High Priest, the only one who stands in the gap between us and God. Here's what the Bible says about that in Hebrews 7:20–28 (MSG):

> The old priesthood of Aaron perpetuated itself automatically, father to son, without explicit confirmation by God. But then God intervened and called this new, permanent priesthood into being with an added promise:
>
> > God gave his word; he won't take it back:
> > "'You're the permanent priest.'"
>
> This makes Jesus the guarantee of a far better way between us and God—one that really works! A new covenant.

Earlier there were a lot of priests, for they died and had to be replaced. But Jesus' priesthood is permanent. He's there from now to eternity to save everyone who comes to God through him, always on the job to speak up for them.

So now we have a high priest who perfectly fits our needs: completely holy, uncompromised by sin, with authority extending as high as God's presence in heaven itself. Unlike the other high priests, he doesn't have to offer sacrifices for his own sins every day before he can get around to us and our sins. He's done it, once and for all: offered up *himself* as the sacrifice. The law appoints as high priests men who are never able to get the job done right. But this intervening command of God, which came later, appoints the Son, who is absolutely, eternally perfect.

That's a big picture to comprehend; yet it illustrates the purpose of Jesus' life. He was a living sacrifice, known as the Lamb of God because there was no more need to sacrifice lambs or anything else after His death on the cross. He took our sin upon Himself and shed His blood so we wouldn't have to do so ourselves. He died so we could live. You don't get a better picture of sacrifice than that. God is not asking us to do something that He was not willing to do Himself first.

You-First in a Me-First World

Someone once said, "Sacrifice is giving up something good for something better." Those who are mature enough to put others before themselves understand this principle. Yet the notion of sacrifice feels like an outdated concept to the world we live in today. Our culture celebrates self-centeredness as strong and declares those who are others-centered as weak. Our celebrity culture plays into this lie fully. The extravagant world the wealthy live in trumpets the message that money is for spending on houses, clothes, cars, and nannies. Rarely do you hear about celebrities who choose to sacrifice their living standard in order to use their money to change the world.

In schools, character values that were taught to help children learn to respect others have been replaced with self-esteem curriculum that cares more about how the child "feels" than helping the child understand how his actions affect those around him. It's all about me . . . me . . . me.

Today's teenagers and young adults are becoming known as the entitlement generation. This generation heads into adulthood expecting to have the same standard of living that their parents had . . . without the hard work and sacrifice to earn it. Child-centered parenting trends communicate to the child that they are the center of their universe. This unfortunately sets the child up to be a self-centered adult who doesn't understand the sacrifice

Good manners are made up of petty sacrifices.

—RALPH WALDO EMERSON

needed to have a successful marriage or be a successful parent. Even basic manners are affected when we don't understand our responsibility to others. Ralph Waldo Emerson said it well when he said, "Good manners are made up of petty sacrifices." How true! The whole concept of manners comes down to sacrificing something as a courtesy to others. God says it this way—"This is my commandment: Love each other in the same way I have loved you. There is no greater love than to lay down one's life for one's friends. You are my friends if you do what I command" (John 15:12–14 NLT). When you help a friend pack boxes to move, it's a sacrifice. When you listen to your teenager lament about her latest crisis, it's sacrifice. When you choose to spend time with your spouse rather than engaging in your favorite hobby, it's sacrifice. When you engage in a conversation with the stranger who tells you about her whole life while standing in the grocery store checkout line, that's sacrifice.

Marriage and parenting require sacrifice that comes by putting others first. When a baby enters a family, sleep must be sacrificed. This little child doesn't have a stomach large enough to consume a meal that will satisfy her for more than three hours. She has to eat around the clock for those first few months. No amount of negotiating will change that. No one will come along and take care of that child's needs besides her parent.

I remember my first few months of motherhood; at the young age of not quite twenty-one. I was barely an adult myself. There were a few tough nights I wondered if I would survive. On those nights I wanted someone to come along and relieve me . . . to take care of me. But I wasn't being sacrificed for anymore. Now I was doing the sacrificing—and it was far harder than I'd ever understood.

Those difficult hours proved to be hours of intimacy with my Friend, Jesus. He understood sacrifice better than anyone else. I would talk to Him in the wee hours of the morning and read little snippets of truth in the Bible whenever I could. It was as if He held my hand and gave me the strength to battle the lack of sleep or the nonstop crying when I was just sure I couldn't take it anymore. When my husband declared that he felt called to ministry, and pursuing Bible college would require leaving friends and family and moving to another state, Jesus reassured me the sacrifice would actually result in relationships deeper than I had ever experienced before. And He was right. When making the decision to stay home for a season of time, my Friend showed me that my sacrifice was worth it. Exchanging my career to be present with my children was a sacrifice with unknown benefits, but one worth taking.

Living others-first in a me-first world is countercultural. It goes against the grain of our self-focused society. It's taking the narrow road when the wide road would be so much easier. But the blessings of sacrifice come down to building character. As you give up the lesser desire for the greater good, an inner quality is forged. When you and I give up a momentary pleasure for a life-enriching experience, the quality of life is deepened until it creates within us a character trait of generosity from which to draw upon. Learning to sacrifice makes us a better person all around. God says, "And do not forget to do good and to share with others, for with such sacrifices God is pleased" (Hebrews 13:16).

Balancing Sacrifice and Self-Care

While Jesus lived a life of sacrifice, He never sacrificed taking care of Himself. He gave His life to others, but never gave up His time with His Father. He ministered everywhere He went, but still took time to eat and sleep. Because Jesus and the disciples walked everywhere they went, exercise was built right into their lifestyle. Jesus was a steward of His body, and that's something we have to learn to be as well. Jesus also never lost Himself in His service and sacrifice for others. He knew who He was, who He belonged to, and what His purpose was in this life.

Sacrifice crosses a line into martyrdom when it's not balanced with self-care. Our kids don't need a martyr; they need a mother. A martyr gives up her life to the extent that she no longer exists—she loses who she is while taking care of everyone else. A mother cares for her family and cares for herself. She allows motherhood to expand her experiences and her understanding of herself. A mother models the art of self-care for her children when she pays attention to her need for rest, nutrition, and exercise. She shows them how to find a Friend who understands when she takes the time to pray and read God's Word. She strengthens their faith when they see her turn to God for answers in her own life. Following the example of Christ we can learn to sacrifice without losing ourselves along the way.

Sacrificial Love

The gift of sacrifice is a gift of yourself. It is the ultimate act of love. One of the most well-known verses of the Bible that speaks of sacrifice is John 3:16 (NLT), "For God loved the world so much that he gave his one and only Son, so that everyone who believes in him will not perish but have eternal life." God's gift of His Son was an act of love.

When we sacrifice, we live out our love. God tells us, "And so, dear brothers and sisters, I plead with you to give your bodies to God because of all he has done for you. Let them be a living and holy sacrifice—the kind he will find acceptable. This is truly the way to worship him. Don't copy the behavior and customs of this world, but let God transform you into a new person by changing the way you think. Then you will learn to know God's will for you, which is good and pleasing and perfect" (Romans 12:1–2 NLT).

This world needs uncommon men and women who aren't afraid to live differently. Two thousand years ago Jesus led the way with His life of sacrifice. Today, may we as moms lead the way with our lives, as well.

Father God, I want Your voice to be louder than the world's voice. But sometimes it feels as if the world is yelling and You are whispering. Help me to hear Your voice clearly as I learn to live a life of sacrifice without losing myself. Thank You for showing me the way with the example of Your Son. Help me to trust Him as my Friend . . . a Friend who understands.

Perspective

I'm dealing with disobedience
around every corner!

Child 1: "I'm in the front seat!"
Child 2: "No, it's my turn!"
Child 1: "Mom, she sat in the front seat yesterday."
Child 2: "I did not . . . you did!"
Child 1: "You always sit in the front seat more than me."
Child 2: "Not true."
Child 1: "Yes, it is."
Child 2: "No it's not."
Child 1: "Yes, it is."

Ah . . . the joys of mothering. Settling arguments. Standing firm. Giving consequences. Being consistent. Correcting. Encouraging. Teaching. The good comes with the bad. The joys with the frustrations. The encouragement with the discouragement. Sometimes your days look nothing like you'd imagined motherhood would be.

...re's a story in the Bible that probably looked something like the above conversation.

James: "I want to sit to His right."

John: "No, I do."

James: "It's my place, I'm the older one."

John: "Well I can handle the responsibility of it."

James: "Mom said it was my place."

I'm taking a bit of creative license here, but I'm quite sure it had some of the same elements of selfish behavior we deal with in our homes. After James and John asked about having the two best seats in the house, the other disciples were ticked off. "When the ten others heard about this, they lost their tempers, thoroughly disgusted with the two brothers. So Jesus got them together to settle things down" (Matthew 20:24–25 MSG). Can't you just see this happening?

I love this wording: "Jesus got them together to settle things down." In the same way that Jesus had to deal with the disciples' immaturity, you and I have to deal with our kids' immaturity. Jesus dealt with their selfishness, their sense of entitlement, and their misbehavior. Sounds like my life. Does it sound like yours?

There was another time when Jesus was frustrated with the disciples. He had taught them what to do but they just weren't getting it. A father requested that Jesus heal his son since he had come to the disciples first and they were unable to handle the responsibility. Jesus responded, "What a generation! No sense of God! No focus to your lives! How many times do I have to go over these things? How much longer do I have to put up with this?" (Matthew 17:17 MSG). Can you hear the frustration in His voice?

Have you heard yourself saying something similar?

Because Jesus wasn't a parent, most of us haven't ever considered that He actually had to deal with disobedience. Sure, Jesus is God and God deals with our disobedience all the time, but what we also see in the Bible is that Jesus poured His life into the disciples—and sometimes they just didn't get it. Likewise, we pour ourselves into our kids, and sometimes they just don't get it either.

I'm going to try and keep this perspective in mind when I want to react with anger rather than respond with self-control in the midst of disobedience. Sometimes a little bit of encouragement from someone who's been there is all we need.

Pray . . .

Jesus, I'm so thankful that You understand what it
feels like to be dealing with disobedience around every corner.
I'm sure there were times when You were talking to the
disciples that it felt like You were talking to a brick wall.
There are times I feel like that, too, as a mom.
Help me know that I'm not alone and
that I have a Friend who does understand.

You get it, my Jesus! Thank You for understanding my frustrations with others and for Your INFIINITE patience with me. Please humble me and help me to remember these truths in the moments I need them most.

Read Matthew chapters 12 and 13.
Ask God to bring His words alive in your heart.

TRUTH . . .

Train a child in the way he should go, and
when he is old he will not turn from it.

PROVERBS 22:6

CHAPTER 6

DISCOVER GOD'S TRUTH:
JESUS FORGAVE

The Truth about Forgiveness

I *now describe it as one of our worst arguments.* During the first ten years of our marriage, Mark and I argued a lot. Usually we both sinned in our anger. We would say things that we'd regret in the morning. During this particular argument Mark said a lot of hurtful things to me. But in a rare departure from my usual behavior, I had refrained from throwing verbal bombs back at him. I was trying to learn self-control and how to fight fair; and on this evening I seemed to have an extra strength that empowered me with self-control. Mark was also learning new ways to handle our conflicts, but this particular evening he had fallen back into old habits.

Mark's words stung as he lobbed them my way. I chose to remain quiet except to calmly communicate my feelings and perspectives and occasionally draw a boundary in our communication. I finally left him in his rage and moved to a different part of the house, refusing to engage in any more of his tirade. We went to bed angry, sleeping in different rooms of the house.

The next morning, a very different man approached me. He was humble and repentant. God had gotten hold of him and he had responded to God's conviction. "Jill, I need to talk to you," he began. "I'm so very sorry for the things I said to you last night. I was wrong and my behavior was wrong. I know I hurt you and for that, I'm very, very sorry. Will you please forgive me?"

Every part of me wanted to lash out in anger. I wanted to say, "Are you kidding? You hurt me. You hurt me bad. Your words were like knives and I'm still bleeding from the cuts you inflicted upon my soul. Do you think you can just come back several hours later, say you're sorry, and put this behind you? You need to pay for what you did!" Those thoughts immediately came to mind as my husband stood before me, but I didn't say them—I just entertained them in my head for a few fleeting moments. The only words I could utter in response to his request was, "Thank you for the apology. I need some time to consider your request for forgiveness."

And the battle began. This time it wasn't between my husband and me. This time it was a battle I fought with myself—and with God.

Forgiveness Is a Choice

As Alexander Pope observed, "To err is human, to forgive, divine." Indeed, I've come to understand that forgiving is something we're only able to do with God's power in our life. Maybe you've misunderstood forgiveness like I have. You've not "felt" like forgiving, so you haven't forgiven. But we will wait a lifetime if we're waiting until we feel like forgiving. Forgiveness isn't a feeling—it's a choice. And quite frankly it all comes down to obedience. God tells us to forgive—and we have to learn to live the way God calls us to live. He knows what's best for us . . . but sometimes it's so hard to do what He asks!

Mark asked for my forgiveness, and his question required an answer. I understood that I had a decision to make, but my emotions were betraying me and controlling my thoughts. I was hurt, angry, and confused. I knew what I needed to do but it completely conflicted with what I wanted to do.

I began to talk with God about it. Okay, maybe it was more of an argument:

Jill: You're asking too much, God.

God: *Trust Me.*

Jill: I want to trust You, but it's just too hard to let this one go.

God: *You're not letting it go. You are giving it to Me.*

Jill: But he hurt me and if I forgive then it is just like I'm saying it's okay.

God: *Not true. You are letting go of the hurt so I can fully have it. You are recognizing that I'm equipped to deal with this better than you are.*

Jill: It's too hard.

God: *I'm not asking you to do something I've never done before. I showed you the way; now follow My lead.*

God's Eraser

Billy Zeoli once said, "God has a big eraser." I would add that God's eraser is far bigger than we can even comprehend. Our relationship with God is based upon His willingness to forgive us. When we come to God with a broken heart, truly sorry about our disobedience or ugly attitudes and actions, His response to our apology and request for forgiveness is yes. It's always yes! God is just, but He is also love, grace, and forgiveness. That's His character and He will not act outside of His character. He asks us to be more like Him . . . and that's where things get hard. In Psalm 86:5 we read, "You are forgiving and good, O Lord, abounding in love to all who call to you." Just a few lines later in the first part of verse 11, we find what our response should be: "Teach me your way, O Lord, and I will walk in your truth." God has a big eraser but He wants us to have a big eraser, too. Psalm 103:10–12 (NLT) describes God's eraser so well:

> He does not punish us for all our sins;
>   he does not deal harshly with us, as we deserve.
> For his unfailing love toward those who fear him
>   is as great as the height of the heavens above the earth.
> He has removed our sins as far from us
>   as the east is from the west.

God does not treat us as we deserve. That's where our dilemma comes in: We often treat others as they deserve. But we forget that we're just as guilty of messing up as they are.

It Starts with Me

If you and I are unable to come to grips with our own need for forgiveness (from God and others) then we can't begin to understand why we need to learn to forgive others. Kay Warren addresses this in *Dangerous Surrender*: "Evil exists in our world; it exists in others, but it also exists in me—and in you . . . By acknowledging our shared depravity and capacity for evil, we can reach out to a fallen brother or sister in mercy rather than in hatred."[6] If we don't take this step, our prideful heart will keep us isolated and unable to really become more like Christ. You and I have to have a heart of humility that comes to terms with our own depravity before we can really understand our need to extend grace and forgiveness to others. First John 1:8–10 (MSG) confirms this.

> If we claim that we're free of sin, we're only fooling ourselves. A claim like that is errant nonsense. On the other hand, if we admit our sins—make a clean breast of them—he won't let us down; he'll be true to himself. He'll forgive our sins and purge us of all wrongdoing. If we claim that we've never sinned, we out-and-out contradict God—make a liar out of him. A claim like that only shows off our ignorance of God.

Unfortunately, our culture doesn't help in this matter at all. We live in a society that thrives on defending rights rather than owning actions. It's rare to find a criminal who pleads guilty. Most look for a legal loophole to secure an innocent verdict, even if they are indeed guilty. Rather than holding their children accountable for their behavior, or allowing someone else (coach, teacher, school administrator) to hold their child accountable, too many parents offer excuses for their child's conduct. Too easily we blame others, defend ourselves, and deny our responsibility in every way we can. But it's time we owned our stuff in our relationships.

Do you need to tell God you're sorry and ask for His forgiveness? Do it today. Do you need to tell your husband you're sorry and ask for his forgiveness? Do it today. Do you need to tell your kids you're sorry and ask for their forgiveness? Don't wait any longer . . . do it today. Josh McDowell says that "forgiveness is the oil of relationships," and every one of our relationships

6. Kay Warren, *Dangerous Surrender* (Grand Rapids: Zondervan, 2007), 118, 120.

probably needs some lubrication that only humility, repentance, and forgiveness can bring.

7. For an interesting discussion of apologies, see *The Five Languages of Apology* by Gary Chapman and Jennifer Thomas (Chicago: Northfield, 2006).

Through counseling, we learned that a full apology is at least seven words: **I'm sorry. Will you please forgive me?**

Several years ago Mark and I realized that we were leaving the forgiveness process out of our conflicts and apologies. When we would have a conflict our apology consisted of two words: *I'm sorry.* Through counseling, we learned that a full apology is at least seven words: *I'm sorry. Will you please forgive me?* This requires a response from the other person that ultimately brings closure to the hurt if they choose to forgive.[7]

When we understand that we make just as many mistakes in life as everyone else, and when we're not afraid to admit those mistakes, we move from pride to humility. God can't use pride, but He can use humility. A humble heart, like Jesus had, makes us so much more available to God.

I Want to Be Like Jesus

The dinner invitation for Jesus came from a Pharisee. Pharisees were known to be hypocritical, self-righteous men who were more concerned about rules about God than relationship with God. Of course, in his holier-than-thou blindness, he completely missed out that by being with Jesus he was actually in the presence of God.

After the guests took their places for the dinner, a woman came to the Pharisee's home. This woman, who had lived a sinful life, possibly as a prostitute, brought with her an expensive bottle of perfume. She sat at Jesus' feet and shed tears of repentance, washing His feet with her tears. As she dried His feet with her hair, He took great compassion on her. He saw that her heart was broken, repentant, and humble, and He forgave her.

That scenario played out over and over again throughout Jesus' three years of ministry. There were different people and different scenarios, but Jesus responded consistently with forgiveness. Jesus not only modeled forgiveness for us, He consistently taught about forgiveness.

Jesus said, "Be alert. If you see your friend going wrong, correct him. If he responds, forgive him. Even if it's personal against you and repeated seven times through the day, and seven times he says, 'I'm sorry, I won't do it again,' forgive him" (Luke 17:3–4 MSG). When teaching the disciples to pray, Jesus asked the Father, in what we know as the Lord's Prayer to "Forgive us our sins as we forgive those who sin against us." And when Jesus hung on the cross the last words He uttered were, "Father, forgive them, for they do not know what they are doing." Jesus lived, breathed, and died with forgiveness on His mind.

Extending Forgiveness

Asking for forgiveness is hard, but granting forgiveness can be even harder. Our sense of justice kicks in and we believe that people need to pay for their mistakes. Extending forgiveness just doesn't seem fair to us. And it isn't. But God's ways are not our ways . . . and when we're on the receiving end of His mercy we can be thankful for that.

One of the misconceptions I used to have about forgiveness is that I needed to forgive when an apology was given and forgiveness was requested. I've come to understand that forgiveness is bigger than that. Forgiveness is how I keep my heart soft, pliable, and sensitive to God's leading. It's more about God and me than it is about anything else. And it needs to happen far more often than I realize.

Let me give you an example of how this happens in a normal mom's day. It's late afternoon and you haven't decided what you're having for dinner yet. You look around and finally decide upon your menu, but you'll need more milk to make your chosen entrée. Looking at the clock, you realize that your husband will be heading home from work in the next half hour so you make a call and ask him to stop at the store and pick up a gallon of milk. He's glad to help out and promises to stop and get the milk on the way home. About one hour later, he walks through the door . . . empty-handed. "Honey, where's the milk?" you ask. He immediately responds with guilt, "Oh my goodness. I completely forgot! I got a call on my cell phone just after leaving the office. The call was an urgent one from Bob at the office and I talked through an issue with him until just a few minutes before pulling in the driveway. I was distracted and completely forgot about the milk! I'm so sorry!"

You may not realize it, but you are at a Y in the road. You can respond in one of two ways: anger or forgiveness. You can lash out at him in anger because he's messed up your perfect plan for having cereal for dinner! (Yes, every mom has done that at least once in her lifetime!) Or you can recognize that there have been plenty of times that you've forgotten to do something he asked you to do and you can offer him forgiveness . . . undeserved mercy. The choice is yours.

I've come to understand that you and I face that Y in the road dozens of times every day. We live with people and people make mistakes. They let us down. They disappoint us. They make poor choices. They forget something that was important to us. You and I have to have a way to handle those hurts and disappointments caused by other people. The way Jesus showed us was to choose forgiveness. The Bible tells

You and I have to have a way to handle those hurts and disappointments caused by other people. The way Jesus showed us was to choose forgiveness.

us, "Make allowance for each other's faults, and forgive any who offends you. Remember, the Lord forgave you, so you must forgive others" (Colossians 3:13 NLT).

Television broadcaster Joan Lunden said, "Holding on to anger, resentment, and hurt only gives you tense muscles, a headache, and a sore jaw from clenching your teeth. Forgiveness gives you back the laughter and the lightness in your life." How true! Forgiveness frees us to love and live without dragging around the baggage of bitterness and unforgiveness. If we can grab hold of that truth, we'll find more joy in life than we've ever experienced before.

It's possible to extend forgiveness to another person without their knowledge. In fact, it's often relationally healthy. In our family we call that "grace space": simply allowing another person to be human . . . to make mistakes . . . and to live in an environment of love, grace, and forgiveness. This creates a home atmosphere that feels safe. It's a place that's safe to fail, safe to make a mistake, and safe to mess up and try something over again.

Forgiveness is not about looking the other way and enabling someone to continue destructive behavior (either destructive to self or others). Continued unhealthy patterns of behavior should be addressed. Jesus wasn't afraid to speak truth to people. He was a straight shooter. But He was also always ready to forgive if the person received truth and had a heart that was tender toward God. You and I need to be willing to speak truth, but we also have to be ready to forgive.

"Forgiveness does not change the past, but it does enlarge the future," observed Paul Boese, a Dutch scientist. Indeed, I found that to be true. Remember the forgiveness Mark requested from me in the beginning of this chapter? After fighting with God for several hours, I finally did the right thing. I chose to forgive. I returned to Mark to answer his question and found that through forgiveness we entered into a new level of intimacy in our relationship. For the sake of the future, both for our future and future generations, let's commit today to recognize the Ys in our road and choose forgiveness more often than any other response. Jesus forgave and we can forgive, too.

Jesus, I want to be more like You, but sometimes it is so hard. Thank You for Your example of forgiveness. You were disappointed. You were hurt. You were betrayed. Yet Your consistent response was forgiveness. Teach me to have a forgiving heart, Lord. Help me to be more like You today.

Perspective

I'm so tired

My friend Julie found herself at the school just a little earlier than usual for pickup. She parked in the car-pool line and began to realize just how tired she was. It had been a long day of chasing preschoolers, and this was the first time she had sat still all day.

With her preschoolers asleep in their car seats in the back-seat, Julie decided to take advantage of the quiet moment, closing her eyes for just a few minutes of rest.

The next thing she knew she startled awake and found all of the moms in the car-pool line driving around her to pull up to the school and pick up their kids. No one bothered to tap on her window and wake her up to move the line. They decided to let this poor, exhausted mom get the shut-eye she obviously needed.

While I've never fallen asleep in the car-pool line, I've most definitely been exhausted enough to consider the possibility. Either we're up at night with a nursing infant or a sick child, up at the crack of dawn with an early riser, waiting up at night for a teenager, or we head to bed later than we should just to get a few things accomplished after the kids are in bed. For whatever reason, most of us don't get the rest our bodies need.

Are you weary? Do you yearn for a nap? Do you fantasize about eight hours of uninterrupted sleep? If so, you're not alone. There are a lot of sleep-deprived mothers out there.

Two thousand years ago, there was a sleep-deprived Savior who lived on this earth. There were days He was physically spent from teaching hundreds and sometimes thousands of people. He often rose early in the morning to pray. There were times when He prayed all night. Not only that, He really didn't even have His own bed. He moved from town to town preaching, teaching, and sleeping somewhere different from day to day. One verse in the Bible says this, "Jesus, tired as he was from the journey, sat down by the well" (John 4:6). That tells us specifically that Jesus felt tired at times!

Maybe you've never thought about the fact that Jesus experienced physical exhaustion. Maybe you've never considered that when you are up at night all alone, you're really not alone. Jesus is with you and He's felt the same thing you have. Just like my friend who was tired enough to sleep sitting up in her car, Jesus was fatigued enough to sleep in a boat in the middle of a storm.

If you haven't learned to nap when your kids nap, consider that to be an important part of self-care in certain seasons of mothering. Sure, you have to let the dishes or the laundry go, but the rest helps you face those tasks with renewed energy and a rested perspective. Don't hesitate to make your needs known. When asked by her husband what she wanted for her birthday, one tired mom stated she wanted to spend the night in a hotel all by herself. Her husband complied and she slept for fourteen straight hours in her dark, quiet hotel room!

Take a few minutes to talk to God about your weariness. Share with Him your struggles, your frustrations, and your constant state of fatigue. Even when it comes to sleep deprivation, you and I have a Friend who understands.

Pray . . .

Jesus, Your physical exhaustion is something I've rarely considered.
Thank You for living on this earth, allowing Yourself to experience
the challenges of this life. When I'm up at night, please help me
remember that I'm not alone. Remind me that You are present
and just waiting for me to have a conversation with You,
my understanding Friend.

I know I'm about to enter this
season of sleep deprivation again,
God, and I'm scared. Please prepare
me and help me to remember
You're with me in the night and
in my exhaustion.

Discover . . .

Read Matthew chapters 14 and 15.
Ask God to speak to you through His Word.

TRUTH . . .

Those who live in the shelter of the Most High
will find rest in the shadow of the Almighty.

PSALM 91:1 (NLT)

CHAPTER 7

The Truth about Leading Our Children

*H*ave you ever heard of the story of the tortoise and the hare?" I asked my two youngest boys one afternoon when we were cleaning the house. "I have but I don't remember what it was about," answered Austin. Kolya replied that he didn't know the story at all. He had been adopted when he was nine and had missed out on many of those familiar children's stories.

Standing in the doorway of the bedroom they were cleaning, I began to share the story about the slow, but persistent tortoise, and the self-assured, but arrogant hare. Austin was overwhelmed with the condition of their room and having trouble staying motivated. I used the story to talk to them about perseverance, encouraging them that big jobs get done in little steps.

Later that evening as I was tucking the boys in bed, I shared with them what Paul said: "I focus on this one thing: Forgetting the past and looking forward to what lies ahead, I press on to reach the end of the race and receive the heavenly prize for which God, through Christ Jesus, is calling us" (Philippians 3:13b–14 NLT). We briefly talked about how we have to persevere in the stuff of everyday life: cleaning our rooms, doing homework, practicing the piano, and more. And then I added that we have to persevere in our spiritual life too, keeping our eye on heaven while living on earth.

There was nothing profound or formal about this life lesson. I was able to tie a story into real life and then apply a spiritual principle. And I learned how to do that from my Friend, Jesus. Just like Jesus, you and I are teachers. And following Jesus' example, we can teach our kids by being storytellers.

Jesus, Storyteller Extraordinaire

Jesus was a teacher, but there wasn't anything boring about His classroom. He was an innovative teacher who used parables, which are short, memorable stories that illustrate a moral lesson. My guess is that if Jesus were a classroom teacher today, students would be competing to get in His class. His stories creatively taught lessons about life, sometimes unraveling the mysteries of God. Yet other times His stories were ambiguous, provoking deep thought and encouraging the listeners to actively listen and engage in the story. Jesus wanted to help people think outside of the box . . . in fact, He wanted them to understand there is no box! Jesus' message was that God can't be contained or compartmentalized—His ways are beyond our comprehension.

As moms we can take our cues from Christ, learning how to use stories to teach our kids creatively. And as our kids get older, we can also use stories that raise more questions than give answers, helping our teens begin to think for themselves. The Bible talks about teaching our children throughout the day in the book of Deuteronomy: "Write these commandments that I've given you today on your hearts. Get them inside of you and then get them inside your children. Talk about them wherever you are, sitting at home or walking in the street; talk about them from the time you get up in the morning to when you fall into bed at night" (Deuteronomy 6:6–7 MSG).

So God asks us to do this, and Jesus led the way, but how do we practically make that happen? How do we teach our kids God's ways in a nonthreatening, creative way? It all starts with you and me and goes from there!

Home As a Church

In my book *My Hearts at Home* I looked at all the different roles that home plays in our life such as Home as a Safe House, Home as a Trauma Unit, Home as a Rest Area, and even Home as a Church. To understand why we need to be teaching our children through stories, we have to first have the vision that our home *is* a church. Too many of us compartmentalize church into what we do on Sunday morning, believing it's the church's job to teach our children spiritual things.

Going to church and Sunday school is one part of investing in a child's spiritual development, but it's not enough. Because more is caught than taught, our children need to see us living out our own faith.

However, there's no way the church has enough time with our children to do more than scratch the surface of teaching them about God. Going to church and Sunday school is one part of investing in a child's spiritual development, but it's not enough. Because more is caught than taught, our children need to see us living out our own faith. Additionally, they need us to weave God's truth in and out of our everyday life activities. That's where following Jesus' examples of telling stories and sharing truth during the everyday activities of real life comes alive.

But you and I can't share something we don't know ourselves, so we have to begin with home being a church for us. What do you do to carry Sunday's church experience into Monday, Tuesday, Wednesday, and beyond? How are you growing your relationship with God? When are you reading the Bible to find truth for your life? When our faith is alive, it's not difficult to share our excitement with our children. But how do we move a stale religious experience into a living faith?

Start with God's Word. Make sure to carry your Bible with you to church on Sunday. When Scripture is read, or while the pastor is preaching, look up those verses and then underline, highlight, and mark all over your Bible to bring the verses alive for you personally.

Read a little bit of God's Word every day at home. We can put a Bible in each bathroom and read just a few lines every time we're in there. If you are nursing, put a Bible by the rocking chair you most often sit in to nurse, then use those minutes you feed your baby to also feed your mind God's truth.

Get involved in an "alive" church family. Our church experience should be empowering and encouraging to our personal faith walk. Find a church that not only has good teaching and a worship style that matches your needs, but also offers Bible studies, a moms group, or other outside opportunities for you to be encouraged in your personal relationship with Jesus Christ.

Talk with God every day. You can have a specific prayer time each day and you can talk to Him throughout the day. Some days

I manage both kinds of conversations. Other days it's one or the other. And on the days that I don't talk with God . . . I know it, my kids know it, and my husband knows it. Mommy's so much of a better mommy when she spends time with Jesus!

Keep Your Eyes Open

Once you are spending time with God, you'll start to see opportunities you never saw before. Your child will be facing a challenge, and a Bible verse you've read will come to mind—don't worry if you can't remember it word for word. Share what you remember to encourage your child in the moment. When I want to find the actual verse, I often use www.biblegateway.com where I can search using whatever words I remember and it helps me locate it in the Bible.

Watch for opportunities in everyday activities to share God's truth. Many times television commercials provide great conversation starters for kids or teenagers. Commercials have all sorts of hidden messages—they are a story in and of themselves. Take a few minutes to dissect a commercial with your kids and then compare that message with God's truth. One family did that so much their kids started calling it the "truth or lie" commercial game.

An example of this might be a commercial that sends a message that anyone who wants to succeed has to have this certain product. You can talk about how the commercial influences the thinking of the viewer by using perfect-looking people and phrases that indicate that you have to have this product. What does God say about this though? There are several ways you could go. You could point your kids toward the Ten Commandments (Exodus 20:1–17) and talk about the commandment that tells us we are not supposed to covet (to want something that someone else has).

Or you could talk about what the Bible says about contentment, which is being okay with what you already have. Let God lead you to see things in a spiritual way and capitalize on the moment. It's not a three-point sermon you need to preach to your kids—you're just looking for opportunities to impart some of God's truth in a relevant, memorable way.

Other opportunities to impart God's truth can be found in God's creation. The land, trees, rivers, animals, wind, and rain all give great opportunity for us to share God's truth with our children. When you see a bird you can say something like, "Did you know that the Bible talks about birds? It says that God takes care of the birds of the air and that we are way more valuable than birds, so we need to trust God to take care of us" (Matthew 6:26). When you see ants on a sidewalk you can tell them that God talks about how hard working the ants are and how we are supposed to learn how to work hard from them (Proverbs 6:6). When you see a rainbow, you can tell your kids that God sent a rainbow after the flood that Noah and his family survived as a promise that He would never flood the whole earth again (Genesis 9:13–15). When you are walking outside on a starry night, you can share with your kids that the Bible tells us that we are to shine like stars in the universe (Philippians 2:14–15).

We can also use personal hygiene activities to prompt God conversations. If you are brushing your child's hair you can tell them that God cares for us so much that He knows the number of hairs on our head (Luke 12:7). When you are bathing your children, you can tell them that when we ask Jesus into our heart (or ask Jesus to be our Friend) He washes away our sins (or mistakes) (Acts 22:16).

You don't have to tie every conversation to a specific Scripture. You can also use life experiences to pass along "God concepts."

For example, when catching snowflakes on your tongues, you can mention that every snowflake God makes is unique and every person that God makes is unique too! There's only one you! When you're taking a walk you can talk about the importance of exercise because God wants us to take care of this wonderful body He's given us. When handling money, you can talk about the importance of using our money God's way and giving God back one penny for every dime (10 percent), which is known as a tithe.

When handling money, you can talk about the importance of using our money God's way and giving God back one penny for every dime (10 percent), which is known as a tithe.

Author Elise Arndt describes this as Devotional Living in her book *A Mother's Touch*. "Devotional Living is the process of conveying spiritual truths throughout our daily experiences. The truths of God's Word are portrayed in the activities that take place in the home. Our senses become sharpened as we begin to recognize opportunities for talking about the message of salvation when we sit, walk, lie down, or rise up."[8]

Elise emphasizes the importance of beginning early with children. Capturing their excitement in the preschool years is a great time for storytelling and devotional living. As children grow into the preteen and teen years their sense of excitement, spontaneity, and wonder begins to disappear. Elise says that you can prepare for the challenging teen years "by establishing devotional living within the home when your children are small. The sooner you start this process the more background you will give them. You are laying a foundation on which they can build their lives."[9] I've certainly found that myself. It's much easier to talk with my teens about spiritual concepts when I've established that as a normal topic of conversation during their younger years.

8. Elise Arndt, *A Mother's Touch* (Wheaton: Victor Books, 1983), 49. — 9. Arndt, 51.

Bringing Bible Stories to Life

There's no reason why you have to find all new stories to share God's truth with your children. Introducing your children to Jesus' parables is just as important. Browse the children's section at your local Christian bookstore to find books that tell the Bible stories in a simplified format. If you have a grade-school child who is learning to read, let them read a story each night before bed. Yes, it takes a little longer for them to stumble over the words, but they will hide those words in their heart when they read them aloud to you.

When reading to younger children, be creative! Use different voices for different people in the story. When reading the story, ask them to point to the pictures of the people you are reading about. Help them to use their imagination and engage them in the story. You can even use hand puppets or small action figures to act out the stories. One mom used movable action figures and farm animals in her children's toy box to bring life to the story of the Good Samaritan (Luke 10:30–37). She said that for several weeks after the story, she'd find her daughter using the action figures to tell the story over and over again to her little brother.

As your children grow older introduce them to the Jesus who walked on this earth. Share perspectives that maybe they've never considered before. I recently had a conversation with my son about a new friend. Kolya was reaching out to Wade, a boy that most kids made fun of. As I tucked Kolya in bed one night I told him that I was very proud of him. He was reaching out to a boy who desperately needed a friend. I told him that his actions reminded me of Jesus. I encouraged him with these words: "Kolya, did you know that you are acting like Jesus to Wade? Jesus would often spend time with people that others wouldn't spend time with. Jesus was inclusive, not exclusive. You are choosing to include Wade and reach out to him even though others make fun of him. I'm sure your actions have put a smile on God's face."

Buried Treasure

Jesus' parables were like buried treasure just waiting to be discovered (Matthew 13:44)! They used the known to define the unknown. His stories were like little dramas that used the ordinary experiences of life to teach about the extraordinary ways of God. Like a skillful artist, Jesus painted pictures of God's truth with short, simple stories. His ultimate goal was not to simply impart knowledge, but to transform a heart from the world's way to God's way.

May we keep that vision in front of us as mothers. With every story that we tell, every truth we share, and every piece of wisdom we impart we're partnering with God to change a heart . . . the heart of our child.

Jesus, Thank You for being such a creative teacher. You have given me so many stories to share with my children. I want to know You more so I can help my children know You more, as well. Prompt me to read the Bible and to look for the buried treasure You have for me. Help me to hear Your voice throughout my day. And help me to see the teaching opportunities that are available to me every day as I connect my child's heart to Your truth.

Perspective

I feel like I'm on display.

It had been a rough morning. Mark and I had started our day with what we call "intense fellowship" (we were arguing!). Our disagreement had stirred up a tense feeling in the house. After a morning with my children, I had everyone head to their rooms for an hour of reading time after lunch.

Since Mark had left for work, I had been convicted of my negative contribution to our early morning disagreement. Once the kids were settled in their rooms, I decided to call Mark to apologize for my stuff and ask for forgiveness. Instead I reached his voice mail, so I left an extended message apologizing for what I'd done and asking for forgiveness. When he arrived home later that afternoon, he thanked me for the phone call and then he apologized, cleaning up his part of the relational mess we'd both made.

The next day, as I was driving our oldest daughter to piano lessons, she said to me, "Mom, I think it was really cool when you called Dad yesterday and said you were sorry." My first thought was, *Where were you when you heard that conversation? You were supposed to be reading in your bedroom!* I decided, however, not to chase that thought. Somehow Anne had heard that conversation, and it had affected her in a huge way.

They say with children more is caught than taught. Indeed, our children are watching us all day. They're "catching" both the good and the bad. Whether we like it or not, you and I are a display of character and values to those God has placed in our care.

But this too is not lost upon Jesus. Talk about being high profile—every move Jesus made was analyzed, criticized, and noticed by someone. If paparazzi had existed in Jesus' time, He would likely have been the most photographed man in history.

Jesus was watched by the church leaders known as the Pharisees. They criticized His every move. These religious men knew how to keep rules, but they had no understanding of the relationship Jesus was offering.

Jesus was watched by His disciples. These men lived with Him, observing and learning every day. Many times Jesus' actions spoke louder than His words.

Jesus was watched by the crowds. He disregarded social classes. Jesus loved everyone equally and could be found in a religious temple just as often as in the home of someone who was considered "unfit" for God by religion's standards.

People were always watching Jesus. And as moms, people— our children—are always watching us.

Those with common experiences find camaraderie when they spend time with others who understand what their life is like. Even if changing the circumstances isn't possible, just knowing that someone else has experienced the same thing gives a person hope for the future.

You and I can't change the fact that we are on display. We have to accept that that's a part of motherhood. But we can find hope and encouragement when we spend time with Someone who understands.

Pray . . .

Jesus, You know what it feels like to live life on display.
Help me to make good choices knowing that my children are watching.
When I make a mistake, help me understand that they can even learn by
watching me respond with humility rather than pride. I want to imitate
You more, knowing that my children are imitating me.

_____

_____

_____

_____

Discover . . .

Read Matthew chapters 16 and 17.
Look for ways that Jesus led by example.

TRUTH . . .

Follow my example, as I follow the example of Christ.

1 CORINTHIANS 11:1

CHAPTER 8

DISCOVER GOD'S TRUTH:
JESUS WAS CONFIDENT

The Truth about Our Identity

*W*e entered the crowded restaurant during the very busy lunch hour. It was a rare occasion for our large family to have the opportunity to eat out, but an unexpected monetary Christmas gift made it possible. As we took our seats, our kids chattered with excitement about Christmas. Anne, who was almost sixteen at the time, was telling me a story about what had happened in Sunday school that morning, and I was doing my best to focus intently on her conversation. Austin, age four, sat to my right and was working to get my attention. Without losing eye contact with Anne, I gave Austin a little bit of sign language indicating that I knew he needed me but I wanted to finish my conversation with Anne first.

Soon the whining moved from "Mommy . . . Mommmmmmmy," to "Mommy, I have to go potty." I again motioned to Austin that I had heard him and would be with him in just one moment. But he couldn't seem to wait. Impatiently he said louder, "Mommy, I gotta go potty. And do you know why I know that I gotta go to the bathroom?" In a moment of exasperation I finally turned to Austin and said, "Okay, Austin. Tell me why you know that you need to go to the bathroom." In his loudest four-year-old voice Austin responded with, "I know that I need to go to the bathroom 'cuz I just farted."

I couldn't believe what he had just said and that he said it so loud. The restaurant went quiet and all eyes focused on our table.

I wanted to crawl under the table, but instead I carefully got up from the table and began to escort Austin to the bathroom. There was one woman over to our right who was visibly offended at what my child said. Then there was a couple over to our left that was working hard to stifle their laughter. I know that my face had to be as red as the Christmas lights that were strung around the room.

Once I was in the bathroom with Austin I began a dialogue with God. "So what do I do about this one, God?" I asked. "I don't know that this was really disobedience as much as it was simply childish foolishness." I continued. "And why do I find myself so humiliated when my children do something foolish in public? This isn't the first time that's happened."

As I stood there looking in the mirror, God spoke to me in that moment. Oh, it wasn't some audible voice that came out of heaven, but rather God brought His truth to my mind to answer that question.

He said to me, Jill, your value and your self-worth is not based upon your children's behavior. Your value is based upon who you belong to. You belong to Me and I love you enough to die for you. It wasn't because you were a good person or a good mom. It was because I love you and you said yes to Me. That doesn't change just because your child misbehaves or says something foolish in public.

Ah, the identity challenges of this world . . . what gives me value? Where do I feel like I belong? Who cares about me? What determines my value and self-worth?

Jesus knew His identity. He understood who He belonged to. You and I have to understand that too.

Jesus' ID

Jesus' life was different right from conception. God supernaturally caused Mary, who was a virgin, to become pregnant. Both Mary and Joseph had angels visit them to communicate who this special child was and what they were to do. It soon became evident to both of them that this child was indeed special.

The first four books of the New Testament serve as biographies of Jesus' life. Matthew, Mark, Luke, and John tell us about the life of Christ on this earth. However, there is little information given about Jesus' life after His birth until He was thirty and began His public ministry. But one story that records an episode that happened when Jesus was twelve years old indicates that Jesus knew His identity. He knew who He belonged to. We find this account in the book of Luke (2:41–52 THE MESSAGE).

Every year Jesus' parents traveled to Jerusalem for the Feast of Passover. When he was twelve years old, they went up as they always did for the Feast. When it was over and they left for home, the child Jesus stayed behind in Jerusalem, but his parents didn't know it. Thinking he was somewhere in the company of pilgrims, they journeyed for a whole day and then began looking for him among relatives and neighbors. When they didn't find him, they went back to Jerusalem looking for him.

The next day they found him in the Temple seated among the teachers, listening to them and asking questions. The teachers were all quite taken with him, impressed with the sharpness of his answers. But his parents were not impressed; they were upset and hurt.

His mother said, "Young man, why have you done this to us? Your father and I have been half out of our minds looking for you."

He said, "Why were you looking for me? Didn't you know that I had to be here, dealing with the things of my Father?" But they had no idea what he was talking about.

So he went back to Nazareth with them, and lived obediently with them. His mother held these things dearly, deep within herself. And Jesus matured, growing up in both body and spirit, blessed by both God and people.

This event is our first evidence that Jesus understood who He was. He knew He belonged first to God, His Father, and He knew that He was to be about His Father's business. Jesus was so sure about what He was to do for His heavenly Father that He lost track of His earthly family as He headed to the temple and they began their journey home.

Don't you wish it was that easy for us? Wouldn't it be nice to have such a strong sense of identity that we wouldn't feel the need to compare ourselves to others, or try to earn approval, or consistently look to our circumstances to help us feel good about ourselves? It is possible, but we have to move off the sand and onto the Rock.

Building Sandcastles

Our favorite vacation spot is at my parents' condo on Okaloosa Island, near Fort Walton Beach and Destin, Florida. Mom and Dad spend a couple of winter months down there and then they rent it out and make it available to family the rest of the year. We've been going since the kids were little so we have many memories of building sandcastles.

The sugar-white sands of the Panhandle coast of Florida make for some beautiful sandcastles. Working for hours in the hot sun, the kids have built elaborate creations well into the evening, only to come out in the morning and find that the tide has come in and washed their structure away. I can't help thinking that experience is an analogy for life.

We work so hard to build our carefully created life. We have visions of being married to a perfect, successful man, living in a house with a white picket fence, and having a perfect family of two children: one boy and one girl. If those dreams come true then our life is good. We feel good about ourselves. We feel good because our family looks good. But that dream can never last. For many of us, it never existed in the first place. And even if your dream wasn't exactly what I described, I'm quite sure that you have some picture in your mind of your perfect circumstances.

But people aren't perfect, so that picture can never last. Husbands will be less than perfect, working an unsatisfying job to make ends meet and still leaving their underwear on the floor even after many years of marriage. That house with the white picket fence will instead be an overcrowded apartment or a house that is much more humble than we pictured in our mind. The pocketbook just won't match the picture in our head. And then there are the kids. They won't cooperate with our perfect dream either. We cannot depend upon our kids to behave the way we want them to in public. Kids are kids . . . they have a mind of their own. They will stubbornly stand firm in their opinion that "they don't want to sing" right before the preschool Christmas program. They will throw a temper tantrum in the grocery store checkout line because you wouldn't let them have a candy bar. They'll want to wear purple pants with a red shirt, socks that don't match, and shoes on the wrong feet. And they won't want you to change any of that because, "I did it myself!"

You and I can't base our self-concept on how our family looks because it's like building our house on sinking sand. We'll work hard to get our "castles" built up perfectly only to have the waves of real life come along and knock the whole thing to pieces. That's what happened to me in the restaurant. My family looked good and I was feeling good about myself. Suddenly one child misbehaved and my whole sense of self-worth came crashing down.

Jesus taught about this very concept in one of His parables. This one is known as the Wise and Foolish Builders (Matthew 7:24–27):

> Therefore everyone who hears these words of mine and puts them into practice is like a wise man who built his house on the rock. The rain came down, the streams rose, and the winds blew and beat against that house; yet it did not fall, because it had its foundation on the rock. But everyone who hears these words of mine and does not put them into practice is like a foolish man who built his house on sand. The rain came down, the streams rose, and the winds blew and beat against that house, and it fell with a great crash.

What I've come to understand is that you and I have a choice. Are we going to build our life on sinking sand or on a solid rock?

A Firm Foundation

Sand shifts. It moves and changes. It can't serve as a dependable foundation. But rocks are different. Rocks are hard. Solid. Unchangeable. They can be depended upon for a solid foothold or foundation.

Too often we look for tangible items to help us feel good about ourselves like college degrees, marital status, the kind of car we drive, the kind of house we live in, or the kind of clothes we wear or our kids wear. Even if we're not attracted to "things" we can easily look to people and circumstances to help us feel good about ourselves. Unfortunately there are consequences that happen with these kinds of pursuits. If we look for things to satisfy us, we can live beyond our means trying to have the things that will help us feel good about ourselves. If we look for people to satisfy us we can become controlling as we try to manage those around us so they will look good and then we can feel good about ourselves. Or we can become shaming in our communication to our husband or children using a tone of voice or words that express how bad they are. We do this to shame them into compliance. And if we don't watch out, we'll base our self-worth on a shaky foundation.

But there is another choice. And it is a perfect solution that will never let us down. You and I can move from the shifting sand to the solid Rock. You see, God never changes. When our value is based on Him it is steady, dependable, and never changing. God is who He says He is. He's the same yesterday, today, and tomorrow. When we look to God to give us our core identity, He'll never let us down. When we say yes to God, we become a daughter of the King. Our name is written in the Book of Life. We are adopted into the family of God and given the family name of Christian—one who belongs to Christ. The problem with the other option is that people change all the time—they're human, after all. They make mistakes. Depending on people or circumstances for our value is like building a home on a foundation of sand. Depending on God for our value is like building a home on a firm foundation—a solid Rock.

Depending on people or circumstances for our value is like building a home on a foundation of sand.

Up to this point I've assumed that you have made this decision and that "Christian" is your name. Maybe you thought you had because you've gone to church your entire life. You did all the "right things" in the church like baptism, First Communion, confirmation classes, and so on. But going to church and even walking through religious ceremonies doesn't make anyone a Christian unless you really understood the words you were saying and embraced the decisions you were making. Those activities give you a foundation of faith for you to make your own decision. God wants your heart. He wants you to accept the gift of salvation by accepting His Son as your Savior. Have you ever said yes to God? If not, then make today your spiritual birthday. All you have to do is pray this prayer or something in your own words that communicates the same thing: "God, I don't want to build my life on sinking sand anymore. Please forgive me for trying to do life on my own. I want to build my life on You, the Solid Rock. I admit that I have done wrong and acted against Your will. Thank You for sending Your Son to live on this earth, and thank You that He understands our human experience. And thank You for His death on the cross that paid for all my wrongs so I can be changed, transformed, given a new life, and live with You forever. I accept Him as my Lord and Savior. In Jesus' name, Amen."

Transformation

Once we have accepted Christ as our Savior, we then begin our journey to let God define us rather than listening to what others say about us. Jon Walker addresses this beautifully when he says,

> Your faith will grow stronger as you focus on your identity in Christ. What this means is that you abandon any image of yourself that is not from God. You stop believing what others have said about you; you stop believing how others have labeled you; you stop accepting how others have defined you.
>
> Where I'm going is here—if you don't know who you are, then you're vulnerable to other people telling you who you are. But the concrete, solid, gospel truth is that you are who God says you are and no one else has a vote in the matter.
>
> You are now identified with Christ and have the power of the Holy Spirit within you. You are God's precious child and he created you in a way that pleases him.
>
> This "identity issue" is an important part of living the abundant life. Jesus was able to face the incredible demands of his mission because he'd settled this identity issue. He knew exactly who he was; he knew that he mattered immensely to his Heavenly Father, and that gave him confidence to move purposefully in faith.[10]

You and I have to know who we are in Christ because that never changes. Here are just a few things that God says about you:

You are a new person! "Anyone who belongs to Christ has become a new person. The old life is gone; a new life has begun!" (2 Corinthians 5:17 NLT).

10. Jon Walker, "Identity in Christ", January 31, 2008, www.christiandads.com.

You are chosen by God! "You are a chosen people. You are royal priests, a holy nation, God's very own possession. As a result, you can show others the goodness of God, for he called you out of the darkness into his wonderful light" (1 Peter 2:9 NLT).

You are an important part of God's family! "All of you together are Christ's body, and each of you is a part of it" (1 Corinthians 12:27 NLT).

You will spend eternity in heaven! "But we are citizens of heaven, where the Lord Jesus Christ lives. And we are eagerly waiting for him to return as our Savior" (Philippians 3:20 NLT).

You belong! "So now you . . . are no longer strangers and foreigners. You are citizens along with all of God's holy people. You are members of God's family" (Ephesians 2:19 NLT).

You are complete! "In Him you have been made complete" (Colossians 2:10 NASB).

You are secure! "[Nothing can] separate us from the love of God that is in Christ Jesus our Lord" (Romans 8:39 NIV).

And that's not all . . . it's just a small peek into who God says you are. God's Word holds so many promises for you and me. The key is that we have to allow His voice and His truth to be louder than anything the world says differently.

You are complete! "In Him you have been made complete" (Colossians 2:10 NASB).

Full Circle

It's been msny years since the "restaurant incident" that launched me into a new understanding of what defines me and gives me value in this life. I can't say that I haven't fallen back into old patterns of thinking at times. But I can say that over time truth has trumped the lies of the world. I've found freedom from the expectations and definitions the lies of the world had put upon me. Most important, I've learned to live my life like Jesus, building my house on the Solid Rock rather than the sinking sand of this world.

Jesus knew who He was. May you and I find our identity and value in the unchanging, unwavering truth of God.

Jesus, Thank You for showing me how to be in the world but not of it. You lived with confidence knowing who You belonged to. I want to do the same. Help me find my identity in You and not in the world I live in.

Perspective

I feel betrayed.

J sat across the restaurant table from a woman I thought was my friend. But now . . . "I told you I wasn't a good friend," she said.

"Yes, you've told me that occasionally throughout the years," I responded. "But I've always found you to be a good friend. I need your friendship," I continued.

"I'm sorry I can't give it to you," she replied. And that was the end of what I thought would be a lifelong friendship. I'd poured my heart, soul, and time into this friendship for over ten years. I had bared my soul. I had trusted her. Shared my heart with her. Conversely, I had listened to her, been there for her, and we had watched our kids grow up together. But in the end she wasn't a loyal friend and even to this day, almost ten years later, the betrayal still hurts when I think about it for any length of time.

Sometimes life hurts. People disappoint us. They let us down. Those we thought were our friends betray our trust, leaving us feeling vulnerable and exposed. Unfortunately it's the price we pay living in community with imperfect people. Which means, of course, it's likely that someone will feel betrayed by us somewhere along the way, too. Sometimes we wound others unintentionally in our imperfect human responses to life.

Jesus lived life in community with His imperfect friends we know as the disciples. They laughed together, ate together, worked together, traveled together, and did ministry together for three years. And even after all that time of building trust, Judas still chose to betray Jesus. "Then one of the Twelve—the one called Judas Iscariot—went to the chief priests and asked, 'What are you willing to give me if I hand him over to you?' So they counted out for him thirty silver coins. From then on Judas watched for an opportunity to hand him over" (Matthew 26:14–16). Judas chose to forfeit a friendship (and ultimately eternity in heaven) for a short-term personal financial gain. His betrayal put into motion the events that would ultimately take Jesus to His death on the cross.

Can you imagine the emotions Jesus must have felt? He'd poured Himself into this man. He'd trusted him enough to ask Him to be a part of His small group. Though as God He knew what Judas was going to do, in His humanity He most likely felt hurt and even disappointed. Jesus had to feel the same emotions you and I feel when someone lets us down.

Time and forgiveness are the only ways to move forward after someone has left a scar on our heart. Many times we'll never fully understand why someone would do something to hurt us so deeply. But talking about the experience with Someone who understands can do a world of good.

Are you feeling the sting from a broken relationship? Have you built a wall of protection around you so tall that no one can now get close to you because of your past hurts? Would you like to find healing, move forward, and know you're not alone?

Don't carry your hurt any further. Open the door of your heart to a Friend who will never betray you. Jesus Christ is the same yesterday, today, and tomorrow. He's felt what you've felt, and experienced what you've experienced. He is a Friend who really understands.

Pray . . .

*Jesus, I'm sure it broke Your heart when Judas
betrayed You. Thank You for understanding the feelings
I've had when those I love have broken my heart.
I know You've designed me to have friendships
on this earth, but I admit that I'm afraid of
being hurt again. Show me how to find a good friend
and be a good friend. And most importantly, help me
learn to trust You more fully as my Savior,
my Lord, and my Friend.*

Discover . . .

Read Matthew chapters 18 and 19.
Ask God to show you what lessons He wants you to learn
for your life from these two chapters.

TRUTH . . .

With man this is impossible, but with God
all things are possible.

MATTHEW 19:26

CHAPTER 9

DISCOVER GOD'S TRUTH:

JESUS WAS TEMPTED

The Truth about Temptation

*J esus was taken into the wild by the Spirit for the Test.
The Devil was ready to give it.* Jesus prepared for the
Test by fasting forty days and forty nights. That left
him, of course, in a state of extreme hunger, which the
Devil took advantage of in the first test: "Since you are
God's Son, speak the word that will turn these stones into
loaves of bread."

Jesus answered by quoting Deuteronomy: "It takes more
than bread to stay alive. It takes a steady stream of words
from God's mouth."

For the second test the Devil took him to the Holy City. He
sat him on top of the Temple and said, "Since you are God's
Son, jump." The Devil goaded him by quoting Psalm 91:

"He has placed you in the care of angels. They will catch you so that you won't so much as stub your toe on a stone."

Jesus countered with another citation from Deuteronomy: "Don't you dare test the Lord your God."

For the third test, the Devil took him on the peak of a huge mountain. He gestured expansively, pointing out all the earth's kingdoms, how glorious they all were. Then he said, "They're yours—lock, stock, and barrel. Just go down on your knees and worship me, and they're yours."

Jesus' refusal was curt: "Beat it, Satan!" He backed his rebuke with a third quotation from Deuteronomy: "Worship the Lord your God, and only him. Serve him with absolute single-heartedness."

The Test was over. The Devil left. And in his place, angels! Angels came and took care of Jesus' needs.
(Matthew 4:1–11 THE MESSAGE)

Temptation Will Happen

Understanding how Jesus lived His life equips us for the reality of our life. This story from the Bible about Jesus facing temptation is no exception. Hearing the stories of other people brings hope and encouragement and often bolsters our faith. With this in mind, one of the most effective parts of a Hearts at Home conference is what we call "My Story." Throughout the year, moms submit their real-life stories allowing us to choose two or three moms to share their stories with the thousands of women at each conference. Some stories deal with the disappointments of life.

Others bring reality to the challenges of life. And still others deal with the temptations of life.

Cheri's story was a story of temptation. As she told her story, I was reminded how easily temptation camouflages lies. The lies cause us to rationalize, which eventually blinds us to truth. Here's Cheri's story in her own words:

> I've been married to a wonderful man for ten years. We have five children, all boys. We've always been very happy in our marriage and I've always found my husband attractive. Both of us described ourselves as happily married and would have never guessed that anything could come between us.
>
> Over the years, I heard people talk about the importance of protecting your marriage. Workshop speakers talked about being careful to not share things with someone of the opposite sex. They cautioned against spending alone time with someone of the opposite sex. Each time I heard those cautions, I disregarded them thinking to myself, "I would never have an affair, we are so happy, and our marriage is so good." I didn't realize that I had become very prideful in my heart. Because I thought that an affair would never happen to me, I let my guard down.
>
> My husband and I attended a small church. We were good friends with one of the couples at the church. In time I began to look forward to anytime I would see this man who was a good friend of my husband. Before long he and I began talking on the phone and eventually he began attending my sons' sporting events. Occasionally I would feel some conviction that my heart was wandering but I would quickly justify my feelings, telling myself that he was just like

a brother and reminding myself that he would even say I felt like one of his sisters. Besides he was my husband's friend. I even asked myself if I was attracted to him and the answer was always no. I rationalized that it was okay and I wasn't crossing any boundaries I shouldn't be.

One day reality hit me and I stopped lying to myself. I didn't really think of him as a brother; the truth was that I was very much attracted to him and the feelings were very strong. Soon after I admitted this to myself, my husband confessed that he had lied to me about pornography. While he had communicated that he didn't struggle with it, the truth was he had pursued it behind my back. Our happily married status was fading away and I was devastated by his confession. Suddenly this other man now looked even better and besides that, I now had an excuse for my behavior and attraction to this other man. In reality I didn't, because my feelings for this other man had developed before my husband had told me of his secret. But in my mind, I continued to blame my husband for my behavior. I used his failure as a scapegoat for my failure.

When I confessed my feelings to this other man, I found that the attraction was mutual. The reality of that knowledge caused me to realize that if he were to show up at my house when no one was home, I wasn't sure I'd be able to say no. That's when fear really set in and I knew that I had to walk in a different direction. I brought my feelings out of the darkness and into the light, not only making this man aware of my feelings, but also telling my husband and the man's wife.

I knew the grass was not really greener on the other side of the fence and I also knew how damaging a physical affair could be, but I could not stop my feelings. One night I received a phone call that I had dreaded would eventually come. He called and said that while it was the last thing he wanted to tell me, our relationship had to stop. We could not continue because we would both be wrecking our homes and our marriages. His wife had been unfaithful at one time and he had worked so hard to get his wife's heart back that he didn't want to compromise their relationship again.

As I faced the reality of what had happened I was forced to reflect upon how I had managed to walk down a path that I prided myself would never happen. That was my first realization—pride had clouded my judgment. Pride had kept me thinking that this would never happen to me—it only happened to others. Pride had kept me rationalizing along the way. When I would hear other people talk about an affair, pride kept me sitting there and thinking, "This is a good story to share, but I don't really need to hear it."

I judged those who had affairs—even those really close to me. I thought my relationship with my husband was safe, but it wasn't. I thought I was guarding my heart, but I wasn't. I had let my guard down and I let the enemy have a foothold into our marriage. I do believe that because of my open communication with all parties involved, I kept it from crossing the line into a physical affair. But the truth is an affair is an affair whether it's physical or emotional. Both do terrible damage to a marriage.

I share this with you out of obedience to God. Quite honestly, it is embarrassing and humiliating to talk about. But God has used this to teach me the lesson that an emotional affair is no different than a physical affair. Sin is sin, and you and I are always one decision away from destroying our marriage and our family. Please don't make the same mistake that I made. Guard your heart and protect your marriage today.

Cheri's story could be your story or my story. In fact, I have a similar story to Cheri's. While working at a dinner theatre when my children were small I became attracted to a man I worked with. Thoughts of him dominated my mind and I found myself enjoying my time at work more than my time at home. I saw only his strengths and my husband's weaknesses. After several months, I too, decided to turn on the lights and get honest with my husband. The affair never crossed the line into a physical relationship, but it did plenty of damage to our marriage. Temptation is real and we have to know how to recognize it and find victory over it.

Understanding Temptation

Life is full of temptation. Usually we find ourselves tempted toward things that are unwise, immoral, or just plain wrong. While sexual temptation often gets the headlines, we face temptation in so many areas of our life. We are tempted to eat too much or to eat too much of the wrong kind of foods. We're tempted to be lazy or let other people do the work if we can get away with it. We're tempted to blame others rather than accepting responsibility. We're tempted toward pride rather than humility. We're tempted toward impatience, anger, and unforgiveness rather than patience, grace, and forgiveness. We're tempted to doubt rather than believe.

Facing temptation is actually strengthening to our faith. The Bible confirms this in the book of James: "Consider it a sheer gift, friends, when tests and challenges come at you from all sides. You know that under pressure, your faith-life is forced into the open and shows its true colors. So don't try to get out of anything prematurely. Let it do its work so you become mature and well-developed, not deficient in any way" (1:2–4 MSG). Temptation forces us to recognize the Ys in the road where we are faced with a choice: Do I choose to proceed my way or God's way? Another way to ask that is, *Am I going to walk in the flesh or in the Spirit?* The Bible says, "Live by the Spirit, and you will not gratify the desires of the sinful nature. For the sinful nature desires what is contrary to the Spirit, and the Spirit what is contrary to the sinful nature. They are in conflict with each other, so that you do not do what you want" (Galatians 5:16–17). The Bible also tells us that when we live by the Spirit there will be fruit, or blessings, in our life: "But the fruit of the Spirit is love, joy, peace, patience, kindness, goodness, faithfulness, gentleness and self-control" (Galatians 5:22–23). I would imagine that you desire those things in your life as much as I do. I want to love more fully and to experience joy. I need patience . . . desperately. I want to be known as being kind, gentle, faithful, and good. And I desperately need self-control! So what the Bible tells us is that if we recognize the Ys in the road and choose to walk God's way, we will experience these blessings in our life. In addition to that, our faith is strengthened and our character deepened.

Another "fruit" that facing temptation brings about is an increased empathy. I've heard it said that temptations and trials are to the spiritual life what exercises at the gym are to the physical life. We become stronger in our faith and more useful for the kingdom.

Consider it a sheer gift, friends, when tests and challenges come at you from all sides.

Having been through the challenge ourselves we are better able to encourage, help, and sympathize with someone who is going through a similar experience.[11] The Bible says, "[God] comes alongside us when we go through hard times, and before you know it, he brings us alongside someone else who is going through hard times so that we can be there for that person just as God was there for us" (2 Corinthians 1:3–4 MSG).

That's exactly what Jesus did for us. That's why He's a Friend who understands! Check this out from the book of Hebrews: "It's obvious, of course, that [Jesus] didn't go to all this trouble for angels. It was for people like us . . . That's why he had to enter into every detail of human life. Then, when he came before God as high priest to get rid of the people's sins, he would have already experienced it all himself—all the pain, all the testing—and would be able to help where help was needed" (Hebrews 2:16–18 MSG). Jesus has experienced temptation, He understands the challenges, and He will walk beside us every step of the way!

There are just two more things we need to understand about temptation before moving on to the strategies for handling temptation. First, it's important to understand the difference between a mistake and sin. Sin has to do with the heart, while a mistake has to do with the head. In other words, a mistake is something you did when you didn't know any better and a sin is something you did when you did know better.[12] Temptation usually entices us toward sin—we know it's wrong, but it draws us in with lies and rationalization.

Second it's important to understand that temptation doesn't come from God, it comes from the Enemy who tries his hardest to separate us from God. James 1:13–15 confirms both of these things: "When tempted, no one should say, 'God is tempting me.' For God cannot be tempted by evil, nor does he tempt anyone; but

11. Christian Wismer Ruth, *Temptations Peculiar to the Sanctified* (Kansas City, Mo: Nazarene Publishing House, 1928), paraphrased concept 2. — 12. Ruth, paraphrased concept 4.

each one is tempted when, by his own evil desire, he is dragged away and enticed. Then, after desire has conceived, it gives birth to sin; and sin, when it is full-grown, gives birth to death." This verse really illustrates what happens when we make a "flesh" choice at the Y in the road. First we are enticed, then desire for the forbidden fruit develops, then we walk in the wrong direction stepping into sin, and then we experience a separation from God (likened to death) because we have chosen to walk our way instead of God's way. But it's not God who has moved to cause that separation. He's stayed in the same place. It's you and I who move away from God by choosing to walk in the flesh rather than in the Spirit. And that's exactly what the Enemy wants us to do . . . he wants there to be distance between God and us.

Spiritual Warfare

Even though I was raised in the church, it wasn't until I was an adult that I began to understand that there was such a thing as spiritual warfare. In fact, I didn't understand that there really was a Devil—I always thought that was just made up for Halloween purposes. But the Bible speaks of Satan many times. Here are just a few of the many names he's known by:

The father of all lies (John 8:44)
The evil or wicked one (Matthew 13:19, 38)
The prince of this world (John 12:31; 14:30; 16:11)
The evil spirit (1 Samuel 16:14)
The power of darkness (Colossians 1:13 NKJV)
The serpent (Genesis 3:4, 14; 2 Corinthians 11:3)
The accuser (Revelations 12:10)
The prince of demons (Matthew 12:24)

A murderer (John 8:44)
The adversary (1 Peter 5:8 NKJV)
Lying spirit (1 Kings 22:22)
The tempter (Matthew 4:3; 1 Thessalonians 3:5)

Satan's first appearance is in the book of Genesis where we find him in the garden of Eden with Adam and Eve. He appeared as the serpent and caused doubt about the instructions God had given them concerning their ability to eat of any tree in the garden except the one Tree of Knowledge of Good and Evil. He's mentioned throughout the Old Testament, but plays a big role in the book of Job. This book tells the story where God allows Satan to test Job, knowing full well that Job is a righteous man and will be able to pass the test. Again there is reference to Satan throughout the New Testament, but one of the most familiar is when Satan tempted Jesus in the wilderness. This is the story I began this chapter with. Since there are hundreds of references to Satan in the Bible, we must conclude that he exists. We can't deny that there is a spiritual world that we cannot see that is active around us. We can also conclude that Satan is always looking for ways to drive a wedge between God and us. His ultimate desire is to alienate mankind from God and God from mankind.

Many years ago I read two books that opened my eyes to the reality of a spiritual world that neither you nor I can see. They were Frank Peretti's books *This Present Darkness* and *Piercing the Darkness*. Though these books are fiction, they are based upon what the Bible says about Satan and his demons who work to wreak havoc on our world. Peretti makes spiritual battles come to life in a vivid way, and at the same time paints a dramatic picture of the power of prayer. The good news is that in the end God wins and Satan loses. But Satan puts up a hard fight on the way, and unfortunately takes a lot of lives and causes a lot of damage. The more we understand that he does exist and how he works, the more we're able to steer clear of temptation or find victory when it does come our way.

Satan is crafty and will often camouflage his lies in such sneaky ways that we don't even recognize them as the lies that they are. I recently talked with Cheri, whose story I shared in the beginning of this chapter. After she shared her story with five thousand moms at a Hearts at Home conference, she had dozens of conversations with women who asked to speak to her during and after the conference. Most of these women told her that they didn't realize that they were being lured into a similar situation until they heard Cheri's story at the conference. They, too, had rationalized until they were blind to the truth. If you'll remember, Cheri rationalized that there was nothing wrong with her relationship with this man in her church. The Enemy whispered lies and she believed them. If we go back to Jesus' example, we see Satan doing the same thing . . . trying to lure Jesus in with his carefully crafted lies.

But what we also see is Jesus' example of how to handle the temptation when it comes our way. Jesus calls out the lies and disarms them with the only antidote for temptation: truth . . . God's never-changing, powerful truth.

Tackling Temptation

Believing the Enemy's lies is like ingesting poison. And as poison does, lies require a powerful antidote to counteract their effects. If we take a look at Jesus' example, we find that the antidote Jesus used is God's Word. He quoted Scripture to undermine the lies.

We need to know God's Word. The Bible is "a lamp to guide my feet and a light for my path" (Psalm 119:105 NLT). We need it to guide our thoughts and bring light to the darkness in our lives!

To be honest, however, I've always struggled with memorizing Scripture. What Scriptures I know by memory have come out of the children's CDs my kids have listened to over the years that have simply been God's Word put to music. When my kids were small we listened to the Donut Man, whose songs were catchy tunes with words straight from the Bible. One song that I can still sing to this day was based upon Philippians 4:13 (NKJV): "I can do all things through Christ who strengthens me." I've spoken that truth many times over the years when I've needed God's strength. One such time was when Austin was a tiny baby. When he was born, he had some health issues that required an MRI. In order to have this MRI he had to lie very still while being moved through a very small tube. To prepare an infant for an MRI you have to sleep deprive him. I did as I was instructed and brought our little guy as sleep deprived as possible (honestly I was far more sleep deprived than he was!). However, Austin just wouldn't stay asleep for the test to be completed. Finally the technician told me that the only way we could finish the test would be for me to go in the machine with Austin lying on my belly. "Are you serious?" I responded with panic. "It's the only way," she answered. The panic continued to rise as I recalled a time when I'd had an MRI myself. Because I am claustrophobic, the doctor had prescribed antianxiety medicine for me to take on the day of the test. There was no pill to take this time. After a brief battle in my mind, I lay down on my back, and the technician placed Austin on top of me. We began to enter the tube belly to belly. He snuggled in and went right to sleep just as I was starting claustrophobic panic. The lies came quickly. "You can't do this . . . you'll never make it through this . . . you can't get out of this machine . . . you're not in control anymore . . . " But just as quickly as the lies surfaced, God's Word came to my mind, "I can do all things through Christ who strengthens me," I recited these words over and over in my mind. To keep my mind focused on the truth, I began to put an emphasis on a different word each time I stated God's truth:

> "*I* can do all things through Christ who strengthens me."
> "I *can* do all things through Christ who strengthens me."
> "I can *do* all things through Christ who strengthens me."

I continued in that pattern until I reached the end of the sentence and then I started all over again. Within a few minutes the panic subsided—replaced by a peace that "transcends all understanding" (Philippians 4:7). The lies were dismantled and God's truth was assembled in my mind. We might not think of a situation like this being temptation, but it is. I was tempted to let fear reign, but God's truth turned the fear into faith.

Within a few minutes the panic subsided—replaced by a peace that "transcends all understanding."

There have been other times when God's Word doesn't necessarily come to my mind so quickly but I remember the general concept of something I've read. I can focus my mind on the general concept, or if I have a Bible or the Internet handy I can look up the actual verse using the concordance (which is like an index for the Bible). When the nonprofit organization Mark worked for many years ago lost their private funding for his salary, I found myself facing lies of fear and doubt. I was tempted to walk in the flesh trying to figure out how we were going to make it financially. I knew there was a verse in the Bible about God's plans for you, but I didn't know where it was or what it said. I went to my concordance in the back of my Bible, looked up the word "plan," and found that the verse was Jeremiah 29:11—"'For I know the plans I have for you,' declares the Lord, 'plans to prosper you and not to harm you, plans to give you hope and a future.'" I read the verse over and over and copied it down in the back of my Bible so I could find it easily. I wrote it on a few note cards so I could post one in my bathroom, put one on the dash of the car, and carry one in my purse. God's truth kept my eyes on the Mountain Mover instead of the mountains during that season of time. And God began to reveal His plans for the future over the coming weeks when He used this as an opportunity for Mark to return to pastoral ministry.

So how do we deal with temptation when it comes our way (notice I said *when* not *if*)? There are several steps we need to take both to prevent temptation and to tackle temptation when we find ourselves facing it.

1. Get ∂resse∂. The Bible talks about putting on the full armor of God, which is similar to what a warrior getting dressed for battle needs. Ephesians 6:10–18 (NLT) explains this:

   A final word: Be strong in the Lord and in his mighty power. Put on all of God's armor so that you will be able to stand firm against all strategies of the devil. For we are not fighting against flesh-and-blood enemies, but against evil rulers and authorities of the unseen world, against mighty powers in this dark world, and against evil spirits in the heavenly places.

   Therefore, put on every piece of God's armor so you will be able to resist the enemy in the time of evil. Then after the battle you will still be standing firm. Stand your ground, putting on the belt of truth and the body armor of God's righteousness. For shoes, put on the peace that comes from the Good News so that you will be fully prepared. In addition to all of these, hold up the shield of faith to stop the fiery arrows of the devil. Put on salvation as your helmet, and take the sword of the Spirit, which is the word of God. Pray in the Spirit at all times and on every occasion. Stay alert and be persistent in your prayers for all believers everywhere.

2. Stay out of tempting situations. For many years my husband and I have had a "spend no alone time with someone of the opposite sex" policy in our marriage. This is just common sense. If I want to secure the services of a personal trainer at the gym, I request a female. If Mark counsels a woman at the church, he keeps the door cracked open or the curtains on the door fully open to the hallway. Set some strategies in place that keep yourself out of tempting situations.

3. Build a hedge of protection. In Jesus' time shepherds built a hedge of thorny bushes around their grazing sheep. This protected the sheep from an unwelcome animal guest helping himself to leg of lamb for dinner. The sheep were protected from an invasion, but the unwelcome guest could still make plenty of howling noise to cause fear in the sheep. In our lives we need to build a hedge of protection around us with accountability from others—living our lives in the light and not in the darkness and sharing our struggles as well as our victories. And we have to drown out the howling lies by turning up God's truth. I find when I have Christian radio on in my car it's very hard for the Enemy to get a word in. I'm too focused on the truth for the lies to slip in.[13] Tackling lies is much easier when done proactively rather than reactively.

13. Ruth, paraphrased concept 6.

14. Ruth, paraphrased concept 11.

4. Use God's truth. Jesus triumphed over temptation by saying, "It is written." His only defense was the Word of God, which is "the sword of the Spirit"(Ephesians 6:17). Human arguments and human wisdom are not enough.[14] We read in Psalm 119:11, "I have hidden your word in my heart, that I might not sin against you." When lies come our way, we have to replace them with God's truth that is hidden in our heart.

Jesus led the way for us to handle the temptations of life. May you and I follow His lead every step of the way.

Lord Jesus, Thank You for leading the way. You don't ask us to do anything that You haven't done before. Thank You for giving me Your strength when mine is weak. Thank You for Your truth that will trump the lies of the Enemy. And thank You for being a Friend who understands.

Perspective

I'm disappointed.

nowing that He was in the last few days of His life, Jesus went with His friends to the garden of Gethsemane. He communicated how distressed He was feeling knowing the emotional and physical pain He was surely facing. He asked His friends to stay with Him and pray. Moving to a place of solitude, Jesus poured out His heart to His Father. After praying for a while He returned to His friends and found them sleeping!

> He said to Peter, "Can't you stick it out with me a single hour? Stay alert; be in prayer so you don't wander into temptation without even knowing you're in danger. There is a part of you that is eager, ready for anything in God. But there's another part that's as lazy as an old dog sleeping by the fire."

> He then left them a second time. Again he prayed, "My Father, if there is no other way than this, drinking this cup to the dregs, I'm ready. Do it your way."

When he came back, he again found them sound asleep. They simply couldn't keep their eyes open. This time he let them sleep on, and went back a third time to pray, going over the same ground one last time.

When he came back the next time, he said, "Are you going to sleep on and make a night of it? My time is up, the Son of Man is about to be handed over to the hands of sinners. Get up! Let's get going! My betrayer is here." (Matthew 26:40–46 THE MESSAGE)

In His moment of greatest need, Jesus' friends were asleep on the job! What a huge disappointment that was for Him. Did you notice the frustration He expressed each time He found His friends asleep?

Disappointment is a part of the human experience. Our husband will disappoint us. Our kids will let us down. Friends and extended family will break their promises. Circumstances out of control will disillusion us. No one can escape the reality of life's disappointments.

How do we handle disappointment in our life? I believe grace is the answer. Grace is something given but not deserved; we don't deserve grace . . . it is a gift from God. When we give grace to others it's an intentional decision we make to let others be human—to make mistakes and not be raked over the coals every time. The more we understand our own need for God's grace, the easier it is to forgive and extend that grace to others.

Are you feeling disappointed? Are you ready to declare, "Hey, this isn't the life I signed up for!"? Has someone come up short on her promises? Don't despair—Jesus understands what you're going through. His friends disappointed Him, but He is the one Friend who will never disappoint us.

Pray . . .

*Jesus, How disappointing it must have been for You to
find Your friends asleep after You had asked them to be there for You.
Life has certainly had its share of disappointments for me as well.
Help me to forgive and give grace when someone lets me down.
I want to be more like You every day.*

Discover . . .

*Read Matthew chapters 20 and 21.
Before reading, pray that God will speak to you
personally through His Word.*

TRUTH . . .

We also rejoice in our sufferings, because we know
that suffering produces perseverance; perseverance,
character; and character, hope.

ROMANS 5:3–4

CHAPTER 10

DISCOVER GOD'S TRUTH:
JESUS WEPT

The Truth about Our Emotions

"*J esus wept.*" John 11:35 is the shortest verse in the Bible. But its implication concerning Jesus' human experience is powerful.

Mary and Martha sent word to Jesus that their brother, Lazarus, was extremely ill. Lazarus and Jesus were friends, and the women knew Jesus would want to know that Lazarus was near death. When Jesus finally arrived, Lazarus had been dead for four days. The grief was overwhelming as the women led Jesus to Lazarus' tomb. When they arrived at the place where Lazarus had been laid, Jesus wept outside the tomb.

After spending some time in grief, Jesus made a request.

"Roll the stone aside," Jesus told them.

But Martha, the dead man's sister, protested, "Lord, he has been dead for four days. The smell will be terrible."

Jesus responded, "Didn't I tell you that you would see God's glory if you believe?" So they rolled the stone aside. Then Jesus looked up to heaven and said, "Father, thank you for hearing me. You always hear me, but I said it out loud for the sake of all these people standing here, so that they will believe you sent me." Then Jesus shouted, "Lazarus, come out!" And the dead man came out, his hands and feet bound in graveclothes, his face wrapped in a headcloth. Jesus told them, "Unwrap him and let him go!" (John 11:39–44 NLT)

What a moment that must have been for those present. They were able to experience the two natures of Jesus: fully God and fully man. Pope Leo I stated: "In his humanity Jesus wept for Lazarus; in his divinity he raised him from the dead."

There's not a one of us who hasn't cried in sadness or grieved the loss of someone dear to us. As we can see here, Jesus experienced those emotions as well. He *is* a Friend who understands.

What Are Emotions?

Emotions are God-given feelings on the inside that motivate us to move in some direction. Anger motivates us toward justice. Joy motivates us to celebrate. Grief motivates us to remember. Hope motivates us to continue on.

God has given us a wide range of emotions to help us accommodate a life with a wide range of experiences. God has even gone as far as connecting our physical experiences to our emotional experiences. For instance, when we feel anxious or fearful our heart rate increases and we often begin to perspire. I remember one occasion when I lost track of my toddler in a department store. She had been standing next to me holding on to my sweatshirt and then the next minute she was gone. My emotion of fear kicked in as I launched into a full-scale search-and-rescue mentality. My breathing quickened, my heart began to beat faster, and my stomach tightened as I walked quickly throughout the women's clothing department. When I finally found her sitting under a clothing rack reciting all of the colors she could see, I felt immediate physical relief.

The psychiatric world categorizes emotions as positive and negative. Positive emotions are feelings like love, joy, hope, peace, or gratitude, and they help us thrive. Negative emotions are feelings like fear, anxiety, anger, or grief, and they help us survive.[15] I believe in God's eyes all of our emotions are positive—because He gave them to us and we are made in His image. However, understanding the two categories of emotions is valuable because our physical health, coping ability, and general well-being are dependent upon living in the so-called positive emotions and only experiencing the negative emotions on occasion. If we live daily in the negative emotions, our physical health will be compromised because we're not designed to live with our heart racing or our blood pressure at such a high level. And when negative emotions linger past their usefulness they produce not only physical side effects but also unnecessary irritability, anxiety disorders, and depression.

Are Emotions True?

It's important for us to understand our emotions, but also understand their limitations. God gave us emotions to navigate both the highs and lows of the human experience. If we think of life as a car, then our emotions serve as the steering wheel of our life, determining the direction we move in.

Dr. David Eckman, author of *Becoming Who God Intended*, says, "Emotions are the music of the soul. They tell you what you are

15. www.psicounsel.com/earlcurley/chapter4.html.

really thinking. When God created music, He created emotion to be its counterpart within us. Like a beautiful melody that accompanies lyrics in a song, emotions are the background music for our thoughts and beliefs. If our beliefs are poor, our emotions will be also. If our beliefs are healthy, our emotions will be powerfully positive."[16]

If our beliefs are poor, our emotions will be also. If our beliefs are healthy, our emotions will be powerfully positive.

What a beautiful description of our emotions (maybe it's the music teacher in me that really connected with that analogy!), but what a powerful picture he also paints with that statement about the limitations of our emotions. While God-given, our emotions require a foundation of faith to keep us in tune with God and His design. You see, our emotions don't always tell us the truth. For example, when you hear a sound in the night and suddenly experience fear, only to find out the cat knocked over a vase in the living room and there was no burglar like you feared. Or when you feel insecure and anxious in a crowd of people and you entertain thoughts like, "I don't belong here. Nobody likes me. I'm worthless and all alone." Those may be your feelings and they are very *real,* but they are not necessarily *true.*

Especially when we're dealing with feelings that have to do with value and self-worth, we need God's truth to guide our way. When we have thoughts like, "Nobody cares . . . I'm worthless," and we run them through God's filter of truth, we find they are not true. God says exactly the opposite. He says "I care" in John 3:16, "For God so loved the world [that's you!] that he gave his one and only Son." And He says in Luke 12:6–7, "Are not five sparrows sold for two pennies? Yet not one of them is forgotten by God. Indeed, the very hairs of your head are all numbered. Don't be afraid; you are worth more than many sparrows."

16. http://whatgodintended.com/content/god-faith-emotions.asp.

The foundation of our emotional well-being really comes down to trust. Do I trust God and what He says? Do I trust my spouse? Do I trust others? When we trust God we allow the Holy Spirit to fill us, guide us, and speak to us. Remember the fruits of the Spirit we talked about in chapter 9? When we let God's Spirit lead us we experience love, joy, peace, patience, kindness, goodness, faithfulness, gentleness, and self-control. (See Galatians 5:22–23.) These are all positive emotions! That's the emotional state God wants us to live in because when we're filled with the Spirit we're spiritually healthy, physically healthy, and emotionally healthy.

Jesus' Emotions on Display

Jesus could be described as loving, joyful, peaceful, patient, kind, faithful, gentle, and self-controlled. Yet we also know there were times that He also allowed Himself to experience anger, grief, and frustration.

We see Jesus' emotions vividly on display in the garden of Gethsemane, told in Matthew 26:36–42. (*The Message* is the version quoted below.) He went to pray there the night before He would be crucified on the cross. "Then Jesus went with them to a garden called Gethsemane and told his disciples, 'Stay here while I go over there and pray.' Taking along Peter and the two sons of Zebedee, he plunged into an agonizing sorrow. Then he said, 'This sorrow is crushing my life out. Stay here and keep vigil with me.'" An agonizing sorrow that was crushing His life out . . . wow, that's deep sorrow. And we think He doesn't understand our emotions and experiences?

The narrative continues: "Going a little ahead, he fell on his face, praying, 'My Father, if there is any way, get me out of this. But please, not what I want. You, what do you want?'" Jesus, in His humanness, was feeling dread. He was dreading the painful death on the cross.

"When he came back to his disciples, he found them sound asleep. He said to Peter, 'Can't you stick it out with me a single hour? Stay alert; be in prayer so you don't wander into temptation without even knowing you're in danger. There is a part of you that is eager, ready for anything in God. But there's another part that's as lazy as an old dog sleeping by the fire.'" Can you hear the frustration in His voice?

"He then left them a second time. Again he prayed, 'My Father, if there is no other way than this . . . I'm ready. Do it your way.'" Jesus is coming face-to-face with truth. He knows that His death on the cross is the only way for God to again have an intimate relationship with the people He created so lovingly.

Jesus experienced just about every emotion that we do, from the level of everyday frustrations and joys to the depths of intensity.

Jesus experienced just about every emotion that we do, from the level of everyday frustrations and joys to the depths of intensity. Understanding this, you and I can do a little self-evaluation. Do I spend more time in a positive emotional state or a negative emotional state? What do I focus on: Peace or anxiety? Love or hate? Forgiveness or anger? Hope or hopelessness? Trust or fear? Our honest answers to those questions will give us a snapshot of our emotional health.

In addition to understanding positive and negative emotions, we need to understand that we often do all kinds of interesting things with our emotions. We turn them on to manipulate others or we turn them off to keep ourselves from feeling something we fear might hurt too much. Some self-evaluation concerning these misuses of our emotions is helpful, too. Do I use my emotions (nonverbally) to get my way? Do I substitute emotions for words? Do I say that things don't bother me, when they really do? By asking ourselves these kinds of questions, we're able to be more in tune with ourselves. The more we are aware of what is happening on the inside, the better wife, mother, friend, and neighbor we will be.

Over the years, Mark and I have learned to pursue emotional health with as much energy as we pursue physical health. In the same way that we exercise our bodies, we exercise our minds by tuning in to our emotions, asking ourselves evaluative questions on occasion, and talking with each other about what we are feeling. When we find that we are emotionally unhealthy with negative thought patterns or behaviors that have lingered longer than they should, we've been just as quick to seek out a Christian counselor as we would a medical doctor. Unfortunately many of us, even in the Christian community, see counseling as a stigma, something that we find shameful rather than healthy. But our emotional health lays the foundations for our relationships, a vital aspect of life. Many moms experience depression, especially after having a baby. This kind of depression is actually caused by hormone imbalance in the body and/or chemical changes in the brain. Depression is when "the baby blues move in to stay." Angie, a mom of four, shared her story about depression at one of our Hearts at Home conferences. Here is her story in her own words:

> I am a strong woman—raised to achieve and excel. I was a good kid, a good student, and a college grad. I am a wife to a busy guy and a four-time mommy. My story begins several years ago.
>
> We struggled with infertility for years. Although the path was filled with sickness, miscarriages, and premature births,

I eventually found myself the mother of a kindergartener, a toddler, and newborn twins. In spite of the blur of those first few months after the twins were born, I was determined to be Super Mom as well as a wonderful wife to my husband. But somewhere along that path, something happened. A part of my soul somehow escaped.

Two years earlier, I walked away from my dream job as a corporate event planner for a Fortune 500 company. I felt God was calling me to give up my ego-fulfilling, stress-loaded job to concentrate on the miracles He had bestowed in my life. I approached stay-at-home motherhood as a change in careers and was sure, like anything else, that I could do it well. I was not prepared for how that decision would change me, change my life, and change who I thought I was. I seemed to be constantly facing challenges and failing at all of them: my stay-at-home "mom-ness," my marriage, my friends, my family. Was this all there was?

After the twins' birth, there was little joy, only endurance. There wasn't living, only surviving. I withdrew and grew angry. My need to stay home turned to fear of leaving my kids and my house. I was overcome with worry and anxiety. I gave up attending my MOPS group (Mothers of Preschoolers) and other activities, and a vicious circle began as people stopped trying to guess what to say and I withdrew more, knowing there was surely something wrong with me. I began to sink deeper and my soul began to shut down. My small, well-meaning little town seemed empty of anyone that would reach me.

My outside still read "I've got it all together." But behind the façade were tears and despair. During those days if one more person had said to me, "Don't you just love staying home?" I would have screamed. But then I did. I started to scream—at everyone: my family, my friends, my precious little children. My life was unraveling.

What was wrong and what I didn't understand was that I was dealing with depression. This is the very first time that I have ever publicly said the word: Depression. Depression is a disease, an illness. Depression is an unwanted guest.

That next spring, I took a HUGE step and journeyed to my first Hearts at Home conference by myself. Well, me and my unwanted guest. The voices inside my head chanted, "This isn't working, you are failing." I sat close to the exit in case I needed to make a break for it. In a room of three thousand women, I felt completely alone.

I was uplifted by the songs and the messages but spent the entire conference in tears. I ignored the chance to talk to someone, to reach out to anyone, to open my soul to the healing it needed. I could distantly feel the stirring, the need to let it all go. I returned home, feeling confused on how to take hold of my life with all of this new information, to be the mom that I saw so many others working to be: happy, content, joy-filled, a godly mother and wife. I heard all of the messages, but I was not ready to let them sink in.

"You are not meant to mother alone, you are not meant to mother alone" seemed to be whispering to my sad, sad soul. I contemplated taking my life. I remember crying to God that I could no longer go on, begging Him to do something. I thought I had failed my family and that I had failed God. Maybe they would all be better off without me.

But God reached into my heart, surrounded me, and flooded me. Before the conference, I had made choices to be alone, to let this loneliness overtake me. But God was waiting patiently. He was there to bring me back—all I had to do was let Him.

God did not give up on getting me back, and so I have you, the women of Hearts at Home to thank. Those whispers of "you are not meant to mother alone" soon began to grow louder, more insistent. Encouraging stories and speakers at the conference, my mother praying on her knees for me, a friend who came by to help or stay, people from church who told me they cared and were praying for me. All of those little acts of kindness spoke great love to me as I began to crawl out of the depths in which I was drowning. It is only by the grace of God and the help of a wonderful professional counselor for almost three years that I am here to share my story with you.

I am a statistic. So are some of you. One out of every three women in this country suffers from depression and a majority of them go untreated. Depression. It moved into my life, my soul, but it has been asked to leave. I'm living proof that you can find life after despair.

This is my story. Do not let it be yours. If you are struggling with the despair I have described, I ask you, for you and for the sake of your family, get the help that you need.

I'm thankful for women like Angie who are willing to be honest about depression and other emotional challenges. And what I love best is their example of seeking help when help is needed. There is nothing shameful about getting the emotional help we need. In fact, much of life is about relationships. We can have the best physical health possible and our relationships are falling apart around us because we won't get serious about our emotional health.

Internal Affairs

Our emotions are like an electrical current running through us at all times. The more aware we are of our internal affairs, the better outcome we'll have with our external affairs. We'll be more enjoyable to be around and more able to handle responsibility. We'll be less likely to get manipulated by our own kids and their misbehavior. We'll be better communicators and better listeners. Emotionally healthy people are more successful in their parenting, their marriages, and their relationships in general.

God created us with multifaceted emotions. Jesus experienced those same emotions. May we follow His lead to embrace our emotions, understand them more fully, and use them responsibly.

Jesus, Thank You for showing me how to live and how to respond to life emotionally. Thank You, God, that You created me to feel. What a wonderful experience feeling really is. Help me to be more in tune with what is going on in my head and my heart. Show me Your truth when my emotions want to tell me otherwise. And help me to love, live, and experience life in a healthy way.

Perspective

I didn't do it!

S he said what?" I responded incredulously to my friend's report of something someone had told her I had said and done. It was a complete lie, and I couldn't understand how someone could create such a fabrication and still live with herself. I listened a few more minutes and then told my friend I didn't want to hear any more.

After she left, I pondered the lie that I'd just learned had been spread about me. It felt like I was back in junior high dealing with the rumor mill of adolescence.

"God, I'm not sure what I should do with this piece of information," I prayed aloud.

I'm your Defender, came the still, small voice of truth in my head.

"That's a new one for me, Lord. I don't know that I've ever considered You my defender," I responded.

Do you trust Me?

"I want to."

Oh, and by the way . . . I was falsely accused at one time, too.

"Thanks for the reminder. I guess I never thought of it that way before."

When I pulled out my Bible I looked up the word "defend" in my concordance, God confirmed what I had just heard Him say with:

> When they cry out to the Lord because of their oppressors, he will send them a savior and defender, and he will rescue them. (Isaiah 19:20)

> Defend my cause and redeem me; preserve my life according to your promise. (Psalm 119:154).

> But make up your mind not to worry beforehand how you will defend yourselves. For I will give you words and wisdom that none of your adversaries will be able to resist or contradict. (Luke 21:14–15)

Jesus is our Defender. He stands in the gap for us before God. He deflects the accusing arrows of the Enemy. But not only that, Jesus understands what it feels like to be falsely accused. In His time on this earth there were many lies spread about Him. The Pharisees couldn't comprehend His ability to do miracles so they responded with, "It is only by Beelzebub, the prince of demons, that this fellow drives out demons" (Matthew 12:24). They said Jesus was an agent of Satan rather than God! That's a pretty big lie. He was mocked on the cross and even called a "deceiver" in the days after His death but before His resurrection (Matthew 27:63). There were so many lies spread about Jesus that any attempt to "manage" His reputation would have been futile. Jesus knew that truth would be His defense. And truth is truth regardless of people's belief or unbelief in that truth.

Someone once said, "A life of integrity needs no defense." That is where I had to settle my heart in regarding this rumor. "God, please use my character to defend me against anyone who might hear these untruthful words. I've certainly made mistakes along the way, but I've tried to live as rightly as possible. Only You can defend me, and I put my trust and hope in You."

Have you been falsely accused? Has someone said something unkind about you to someone else? If so, you're not alone. Jesus experienced the same things Himself. He not only understands the feelings, but He's willing to be our Protector and Defender if we'll move aside and let Him do His job.

Pray . . .

Jesus, It makes me feel helpless when I'm unable to set the record straight sometimes. However, I know that feeling comes from trying to do things on my own. Help me to trust You as my Defender. You've faced horrendous accusations— may I never forget that You do know what I'm feeling and You'll never abandon me even in my most difficult moments of life.

Discover . . .

Read Matthew chapters 22 and 23.

Before reading pray that God would open

the eyes of your heart to His truth.

TRUTH . . .

"Love the Lord your God with all your heart and
with all your soul and with all your mind." This is the
first and greatest commandment.

MATTHEW 22:37–38

CHAPTER 11

The Truth about Prayer

*A*s I folded Mark's T-shirt I began my conversation with God. "God, thank You for my husband. Thank You for all that You have created him to be." I smoothed out a pair of jeans with, "Lord, help him to look to You for his value rather than his job or what the world falsely offers. I pray that he will be a man who longs for Your truth." As I began to pair his socks I prayed, "Keep his feet on Your path, Lord. Help him to walk in the Spirit more often than in the flesh."

As I pulled a couple of Erica's shirts out of the laundry basket, I prayed, "Lord, help Erica to want what You offer more than what the world has to offer. Keep her strong against the peer pressure she experiences in high school."

A couple of pairs of jeans belonging to Austin were next on the pile: "Lord, he's eleven and trying to find his niche in the world. I pray against the lies of the Enemy that would cause him to look for acceptance from the wrong places."

Kolya's jeans were next. "Lord, Kolya still has baggage from nine years in an orphanage. Show me his emotional needs and how to best meet them."

A couple of my pieces of clothing were next in the laundry basket. "God, I need Your direction for creating a moms group at our new church. Is that something You want me to do? Please either open or shut the door on that possibility." I finished up the load of laundry by thanking God for a husband and children who have blessed my life.

Prayer has revolutionized my life and my laundry!

Communicating with God

Did you know that prayer is just having a conversation with God? Too often we get so focused on the "religion" part of things that we miss the relationship piece it's designed to be. There's no right or wrong way to pray, any more than there is a right or wrong way to have a conversation with a friend. Our friendships reflect our personalities and our friendship with God is no different. In the same way, however, a friendship is also made up of many kinds of conversations. There's the quick "Hey, how are you doing?" conversation you might have in a five-minute phone call. Then there is the "I need your advice" conversation when one person asks another for wisdom. And then there are the deep, honest conversations that happen when two people really bare their souls to each another. All of these conversations make up a friendship and all are also needed in our friendship with God.

God wants us to talk with Him and He also desires to speak to us. He longs for a relationship, and a true relationship can never be one-sided. We speak and He listens. We listen and He speaks. But how do we do that? How do we learn to speak comfortably with God? How do we learn to hear His voice?

Once again, Jesus leads the way. Jesus spent a large amount of time praying. He was building intimacy with His father, seeking direction, and finding spiritual strength for the journey. We need the same things and that's why we need to pray! Let's take a look at Jesus' example and answer these questions about prayer: Where? When? Why? How?

Where?

When looking at Jesus' life as it pertains to prayer, one of the first things I noticed was that we never see Jesus praying in a religious meeting or synagogue or even publicly very often, for that matter. He may very well have and it's just not recorded, but we can conclude that Jesus prayed more often outside of a public setting and usually moved away from distractions so He could focus on God. We read about Him praying wherever He was: on a mountain, in a river, in a garden, or what is often referred to as "a solitary place." Here are some of the places we see this in the Bible:

> Jesus went out to a mountainside to pray, and spent the night praying to God. (Luke 6:12)

> After all the people were baptized, Jesus was baptized. As he was praying, the sky opened up and the Holy Spirit, like a dove descending, came down on him. (Luke 3:21–22 MSG)

> Then Jesus went with them to a garden called Gethsemane and told his disciples, "Stay here while I go over there and pray." (Matthew 26:36)

> Very early in the morning, while it was still dark, Jesus got up, left the house and went off to a solitary place, where he prayed. (Mark 1:35)

What that models for us is that our prayer life is something that happens outside of Sunday morning church. We certainly pray at church, but more important, prayer needs to be a part of our everyday life. Jesus showed us that we need to live life with an attitude of prayer—which really means being aware of the presence of God at all times.

So how does a mom follow Jesus' example? She prays throughout her day, inspired by whatever she's doing! That's how I revolutionized doing laundry, washing dishes, cleaning house, and even running a car pool. I turned my tasks into prayer prompts, using my family's clothing, car, and home environment as an inspiration to pray.

Watching my kids play at the park might prompt a moment of thankfulness. "God, Thank You for these beautiful children You've given me. Thank You for their unique personalities." While enjoying a performance by Anne, Evan, or Erica on stage in a musical or piano recital I've taken a few moments to chat with the Lord: "Father, Thank You for the unique talents You've given my child. Help me to find a perfect balance to encourage, but not control or push." While Austin played baseball and Kolya ran track I prayed, "God, Please put Your hand of protection on my son. I pray that this would give him physical strength, but most importantly I pray for his character. May he see that winning in the world and winning in Your eyes are completely different things. I pray that he will want to please You more than anyone in this world." These have been silent prayers just between me and God, but they've been heartfelt, honest prayers from the heart of a mother.

Everyday life gives us so many opportunities to bless our family; pray for wisdom, protection, and direction; and just spend time talking with God. Some of these same situations can also be prompts to listen. You can turn on a Christian radio station and let

God speak to you through the music when it's your turn to drive the car pool. Whisper, "God, I want to hear Your voice. Bring Your truth to my mind. Lead my eyes to see Your creation with fresh eyes today" while you're sitting on a park bench watching your kids play. One time when I was praying that very way, I suddenly noticed the birds scattered throughout the park. I hadn't taken a close look at them before. There were different shapes, sizes, and colors. God reminded me of this verse in the Bible—"Are not five sparrows sold for two pennies? Yet not one of them is forgotten by God. Indeed, the very hairs of your head are all numbered. Don't be afraid; you are worth more than many sparrows" (Luke 12:6–7). I didn't remember the exact wording of the verse or even where it was in the Bible, but I remembered the concept. In that moment God spoke to me about my value to Him. There was no voice from heaven, no parting of the clouds, and the awareness lasted all of about two minutes. But it grounded me in truth and brought an internal peace I desperately needed after an exhausting afternoon of mothering.

> *God, I want to hear Your voice. Bring Your truth to my mind. Lead my eyes to see Your creation with fresh eyes today.*

Jesus prayed spontaneously . . . I like to call those "snacks with God." But He also prayed intentionally . . . and those times are like having a meal with God. A vibrant, growing relationship needs both kinds of interactions. Somewhere along my mothering journey I heard a speaker suggest creating a "prayer basket" that helps with those intentional mealtimes with God. You can create a basket that holds all your tools—Bible, a prayer journal, and a devotional. I also keep note cards in my basket to write a note to a friend that God has prompted me to pray for on any particular day. A meal with God could be as short as five to ten minutes when your kids are entertaining themselves, to twenty minutes or more during their nap time.

There are many times when I sit down to chat with God I find myself feeling weary. Instead of fighting the feeling, I close my eyes and take a little nap myself. Jesus understands. He grew tired too!

I've also learned to keep my "to do" list with me during my mealtimes with God. It seems when I slow down to read the Bible and talk to God, I begin to think of all the things I need to do: thaw the hamburger for dinner, call and reschedule a dentist appointment, or pick up the dry cleaning I forgot. Instead of trying to mentally keep a list in my head that distracts me from my time with God, I simply jot those things down so my mind is free to focus on God.

Whether you're in the bedroom folding laundry, in the kitchen making dinner, in your favorite recliner in the family room, or in the car on your way to pick up the kids from school, a vibrant prayer life can revolutionize any activity. God is ready, available, and waiting to talk to us at any time during the day.

So where does a mom pray? Wherever she is!

When?

"Jesus went out as usual to the Mount of Olives, and his disciples followed him. On reaching the place, he said to them, 'Pray that you will not fall into temptation'" (Luke 22:39–40). When I read this verse about Jesus' prayer life, two words jump out at me: as usual. This was a regular routine for Jesus. Oh, how I want that in my life! I want my kids to be able to say, "Mom's out talking to God on the porch, as usual." Or "Mom's in the living room with her Bible, as usual." Or "As usual, mom's writing in her journal to God while we're having our rest time."

I know I have to cut myself some slack because there's little in motherhood that runs *as usual*. Every day, in fact every moment, is full of surprises! You and I have to expect that and be willing to ride the roller coaster of motherhood with our hands held high over our head. There are twists and turns that will mess with the best-laid plans. However, I must admit there are many days that intentionally spending time with God doesn't even cross my mind. I become too task centered. I let myself react to my day rather than letting God lead me through my day. I fill my hours with dentist, orthodontist, and doctor appointments and don't even pencil in an appointment with God.

Yet God waits . . . longing for me, and for you, to spend time with Him. He has gifts for you and me that remain wrapped and unopened: peace, joy, patience, and truth. He wants to hear our hearts and share His heart with us.

Jesus was busy, but He was never too busy to pray. That's what I want in my life. I'm a busy mom. But I want to never be too busy to pray. This is one area where I long to be more like Jesus Christ and model my praying after His—and once again take my cues from Him.

When Jesus went to Lazarus' tomb and made the decision to raise him from the dead, He prayed because there was a need. "So they rolled the stone aside. Then Jesus looked up to heaven and said, 'Father, thank you for hearing me. You always hear me, but I said it out loud for the sake of all these people standing here, so that they will believe you sent me'" (John 11:41–42 NLT). Jesus needed to thank God for the miracle He was about to perform. He needed to give God the glory publicly.

When Jesus needed strength He prayed. Just days from His death on the cross, Jesus "prayed that, if it were possible, the awful hour awaiting him might pass him by. 'Abba, Father,' he cried out, 'everything is possible for you. Please take this cup of suffering away from me. Yet I want your will to be done, not mine'" (Mark 14:35–36 NLT). Jesus was weary. He needed to pour out His heart to God. He submitted His flesh—His life—to God. Oh, how often

I need to do that! I've prayed that kind of prayer when I've faced a hard decision or a difficult conversation or when I've wanted to hang on rather than let go of my maturing children. But I need to do it more often.

We know that a relationship with God is a two-way street. Jesus spent many hours—even an entire night—praying. That kind of time isn't spent just talking to God; it's spent listening and receiving direction as well. God speaks to us through His Word (the Bible) and through the Holy Spirit. There have been many times that I've missed God's promptings and other times I've recognized them and responded appropriately. I remember one time specifically when I got it right.

We know that a relationship with God is a two-way street.

When Mark and I purchased our hundred-year-old farm-house, we had so much renovation to do that we couldn't even think about what to do with an eight-by-ten foot hole that had a poured-concrete lining in our side yard. Two years after moving in we started talking about making the now-cracked concrete hole into a pond. After much research, we sadly determined that making even a small pond just wasn't in our budget. The cost of the lining, filters, rocks, and plants was simply too expensive. One morning when I was sitting out on the deck, God spoke to my heart, *Jill, you haven't prayed for a pond.* It was true. We had not even considered asking God for what seemed like such a trivial, yet extravagant, desire. This wasn't a need . . . it definitely fell into the "want" category.

When Mark came home that night I shared with him what God had impressed on my heart. We agreed to pray and see what God has in store for us. Two weeks after we started praying, I was reading our local newspaper and happened upon a column called "Good Neighbors" where people can advertise items they want to give away. My eye caught these words: "I have a backyard pond to give away. Must be willing to dismantle." I couldn't believe my eyes! I ran to Mark and showed him the paper. He encouraged me to write a response right away.

"Good Neighbors" posts items without any contact information. If someone is interested in the item offered, they write to the newspaper. The responses are then posted with contact information, and it becomes the responsibility of the first party to call those interested and arrange for a give-away of the item.

I wrote to the newspaper and indicated our interest. Several days later I opened up the paper and found the column. There was our response and contact information . . . with about fifteen others who were also interested! My heart dropped. Our post was about halfway down the list. If the pond owner started at the top, she'd surely give it to one of the first few responses listed. I sighed and prayed, "God, it's in Your hands. If this pond is meant for us, please lead the way. If not, please give us a peace about the whole thing."

Later that evening, the phone rang. "Hi," said an unfamiliar voice. "I'm the one with the pond to give away. Are you still interested?"

"Yes!" I responded. "We've been praying for a pond and we'd love to have it!"

"Well," she answered excitedly, "I was overwhelmed when I saw all the responses and I didn't know what to do, so I prayed too, and God really drew my eyes to your response." We both marveled at God's direction in the whole situation. After a brief conversation, she gave me her address and we scheduled a time that our family would come over and dismantle the pond in her backyard that she no longer wanted to maintain. Today our "God Pond" is a visual reminder of God's ability to speak to us and prompt us to pray. It's also a reminder that God cares about our wants as well as our needs.

Jesus intentionally set aside time to spend with His heavenly

Father. Sometimes He went alone: "Very early in the morning, while it was still dark, Jesus got up, left the house and went off to a solitary place, where he prayed" (Mark 1:35). And other times He took His friends, the disciples, with Him: "Jesus . . . took Peter, John and James with him and went up onto a mountain to pray" (Luke 9:28).

Have you ever noticed how you become more like your friends the more you spend time with them? You start using the same phrases. Your pick up some of their inflections of speech. Or maybe you've noticed it more with your kids—they are more sassy or argumentative after spending time with a certain friend. The influence can be positive or negative, but the truth is, we become like those we hang with.

The same is true with God. If we are hanging with God we'll become more like Him! That's a positive influence in my life and I definitely want that for my kids, too! Making an appointment with God each day helps us to be intentional about spending time with Him. But when should that happen? Should it always be first thing in the morning? Is this what people are referring to when they say they have a daily "quiet time"?

Time with God, often referred to in Christian circles as a "quiet time," could happen in the best part of your day. If you are a morning person, that would be in the morning. If you're nocturnal, you might find that an afternoon or evening time with God would work better for you. There's no right or wrong time of day—Jesus had His "quiet time" at different times of the day. The Bible says that "one of those days Jesus went out to a mountainside to pray, and spent the night praying to God" (Luke 6:12). This indicates that Jesus spent time with God during the day and even throughout an entire night. Mark 1:35, as we just read, tells us that sometimes Jesus got up and prayed "very early in the morning."

Your quiet time could also be a discipline you choose to pursue. I know several people who are not morning people, but they choose to get up early and have some time with God before beginning their day. Every time I tried that it seemed that my kids got up earlier and earlier, too! But I also learned to see the positive side of that. When they'd come down the stairs and find me sitting in a chair with my Bible, my example spoke louder than my words. Sometimes they would cuddle up in my lap and I would read a few verses aloud to them.

I find a late-morning appointment with God works best for me. Once I get the kids out the door to school, I head to the gym. Then I return home to shower and have my quiet time to begin my day. Some days that schedule works well and other days I find it more challenging.

Jesus sometimes took His friends with Him to pray. I would liken that experience to the prayer time I have with my Moms In Prayer group. Moms In Prayer International impacts children and schools worldwide for Christ by gathering mothers to pray.[17] I started praying with other moms when our oldest daughter, Anne, started kindergarten. I was honestly more worried about her riding the school bus than I was about her going to kindergarten. But I decided to take my worries to God. This one-hour-a-week commitment changed my prayer life! I went into Moms In Prayer wondering how anyone could pray for an entire hour. I soon learned, however, just how much there is to talk to God about when you are praying for your kids and their school. If you'd like to see if there's a Moms In Prayer group near you, check out www.momsinprayer.org.

God's not picky about when you spend time with Him—it may be first thing in the morning, during nap time in the afternoon, or before you go to bed. He just wants you to spend time with Him!

17. This is the Moms In Touch mission statement found at www.momsintouch.org.

When should you pray? Whenever there's a need, whenever God prompts you, or whenever you plan to spend time with Him. Any time is the right time to spend time with God.

Why?

If you're not convinced of the importance of prayer, when and where will never matter. Why should we pray? What happens when we pray? Why is prayer so important? The answers to these questions will serve as the foundation for our prayer life.

When we spend time with a friend, we deepen the intimacy of the friendship. One reason we pray is to deepen our intimacy with God. God wants to hear our hearts, but He also longs for us to know His heart. Many times we'll see God through the filter of our experience with our earthly father. But rarely does that give us an accurate, balanced picture of who God really is. The more we spend time with Him, the more we learn about His character. And ultimately that builds trust—one of the most important parts of any lasting relationship. Jesus spent enough time with God to trust His plan for Him to die on the cross for us. That's a lot of trust!

Do you ever feel that something is absolutely impossible? Maybe it's a relationship that needs to change or circumstances that are beyond your control. It could be physical or financial needs. Prayer is what changes something from "mission impossible" to "mission possible." Why? Because prayer unlocks God's power in your life. God's power can change nature, circumstances, and people's hearts. The Bible tells us of many incidents where God's power changed what would have been considered impossible. When a terrible storm

> Prayer unlocks God's power in your life. God's power can change nature, circumstances, and people's hearts.

caused great fear and put the disciples in danger, Jesus calmed the storm (Mark 4:35–41). When Peter was in prison, God caused the chains to fall off Peter's wrists and sent an angel to rescue him from prison (Acts 12:6–17). When Saul was traveling down a road, God changed him—an outspoken persecutor of Christians, into Paul—one of the most effective preachers of God's truth. (Read the story of Paul's conversion in Acts 9:1–31.) Nothing is impossible with God! And when you and I pray, the impossible becomes possible in our lives.

Another reason we pray is to do battle in the spiritual world. Remember our chapter on temptation? There is a spiritual battle of good and evil going on around us all the time. We can't see it, but we can learn to recognize it. And we have to remember that prayer is a weapon we can use to fight against the Enemy's ploys to deceive. Ephesians 6:10–12 and 18 addresses this:

> Finally, be strong in the Lord and in his mighty power.
> Put on the full armor of God so that you can take your
> stand against the devil's schemes. For our struggle is not
> against flesh and blood, but against the rulers, against the
> authorities, against the powers of this dark world and
> against the spiritual forces of evil in the heavenly realms.
> . . . And pray in the Spirit on all occasions with all kinds of
> prayers and requests. With this in mind, be alert and always
> keep on praying for all the saints.

Prayer increases our intimacy with God, it opens a channel for God's power in our lives, and it is a powerful weapon against the spiritual battles in our life. Someone once said when we work, we work, but when we pray, God works. I'm willing to bet that you want God to work in your life as much as I do. Prayer is the key to making that happen.

So why should we pray? Because God is able, generous, strong, powerful, available, just, forgiving, and He longs for us to allow Him full access to our hearts and our lives!

How?

Sometimes our prayers can end up sounding more like a shopping list than a heartfelt conversation. As humans we have a bad case of the "gimme" bug. Gimme more patience, please God. Gimme this job. Gimme a way out of this situation. If you do, I'll _____. That's when the "gimmes" move into bargaining: if you do this, God, then I'll do that. Our default prayers happen simply because we don't know any different. But Jesus never fails us. Again, He showed us the way.

> One day Jesus was praying in a certain place. When he finished, one of his disciples said to him, "Lord, teach us to pray, just as John taught his disciples." He said to them, "When you pray, say:
>
> "'Our Father in heaven, may your name be kept holy.
> May your Kingdom come soon.
> May your will be done on earth, as it is in heaven.
> Give us today the food we need,
> and forgive us our sins, as we have forgiven those
>   who sin against us.
> And don't let us yield to temptation, but rescue us
>   from the evil one.'"

You and I may know this as the Lord's Prayer, which is often recited in church services each Sunday. What we see, however, is

(These passages are taken from Luke 11:1–4 and Matthew 6:9–13).

that this wasn't some prayer we were to repeat as much as it was an example Jesus gave while He was teaching the disciples how to pray. By looking closely at this prayer, we can learn how to pray more fully.

"Our Father in heaven, may your name be kept holy." Jesus instructs us to begin our prayers by giving praise and adoration to God. When we do this we concentrate solely on God, taking our eyes off ourselves and putting them on God. Doing this purifies our hearts and gets us in a right place before God. It also gives God the glory He deserves and focuses on who God is. I find there are two phrases that keep me focused on adoration: "God I praise you because you are _____." Or simply "God, you are _____." The blanks are filled in with words that describe God such as forgiving, worthy, powerful, hope, love, joy, peace, kind, just, truth, all-knowing, and more! After giving praise to God, we need to thank Him for His work in our lives. This too is giving God the glory He deserves. Too often we pray and then forget to say "thank You" for answered prayers.

"May your Kingdom come soon. May your will be done on earth, as it is in heaven." We need to pray for God's will over our will recognizing that He has the ability to see the whole context of any situation. You and I are limited in our perspective. But God has no limitations. He is all-knowing and we have to learn to trust that He has the big picture in mind.

"Give us today the food we need." God wants us to ask Him for what we need. He wants us to bring our hopes, desires, needs, and wants to Him. I love how *The Message* words Luke 11:9–13:

Here's what I'm saying:
Ask and you'll get;
Seek and you'll find;
Knock and the door will open.

Don't bargain with God. Be direct. Ask for what you need. This is not a cat-and-mouse, hide-and-seek game we're in. If your little boy asks for a serving of fish, do you scare him with a live snake on his plate? If your little girl asks for an egg, do you trick her with a spider? As bad as you are, you wouldn't think of such a thing—you're at least decent to your own children. And don't you think the Father who conceived you in love will give the Holy Spirit when you ask him?

And forgive us our sins, as we have forgiven those who sin against us. Here Jesus is telling us that confession is an important part of prayer. We need to call our sins what they are, own them, and ask for forgiveness. This cleans up our conscience and allows us to feel the relief of God's grace and forgiveness. More importantly, however, we are more likely to experience change in our lives when we are totally honest about our sins.

And don't let us yield to temptation, but rescue us from the evil one. This brings us back to the importance of praying against the work of the enemy. If we don't recognize the temptation that Satan presents, we'll fall for it. Prayer builds up our arsenal of weapons to fight the enemy.

The Power of Prayer

Bill Hybels states in his book *Too Busy Not to Pray*, "Prayer is an unnatural activity. From birth we have been learning the rules of self-reliance as we strain and struggle to achieve self-sufficiency. Prayer flies in the face of those deep-seated values. It is an assault on human autonomy, an indictment of independent living. To people in the fast lane, determined to make it on their own, prayer is an embarrassing interruption. Prayer is alien to our proud human nature. And yet somewhere, someplace, probably all of us reach the point of falling to our knees, bowing our heads, fixing our attention on God and praying."[18]

I agree with Hybels, but I've also found that God is in the business of changing the unnatural in our lives to natural. He's all about creating a "new normal" for us as we travel along this journey of faith. One can't come in contact with the God of the universe and not be changed in some way.

May you and I follow Jesus' example and make prayer a priority in our life.

Lord, I want to deepen my relationship with You. Help me to think about prayer in a different way—a way that opens up the communication lines so that I know You better and I'm able to share my heart more freely, building trust along the way. Thank You, Jesus, for leading by example and showing me the way.

18. Bill Hybels, *Too Busy Not to Pray* (Downers Grove, Ill.: InterVarsity Press, 1988), 7.

Perspective

*There's never enough money,
time, or me to go around!*

J wish we had cable television," complained my husband one summer evening several years ago. "I know, there are times that I wish we did, too," I responded. For most of our marriage it seems like there's always been more month at the end of the money. We've lived as frugally as possible, but the reality of having a large family on a pastor's modest income has been extremely challenging.

Several years ago, I had an opportunity to travel to El Salvador with Compassion International. It was a sobering experience as I had never seen such poverty in my entire life. On the last night of our trip, one of our trip leaders asked a question that I keep tossing around in my head. He asked: "What is the opposite of poverty?"

Most of us would answer that question with, "wealth." Wealth seems to be the logical response. But it isn't the answer. Wes Stafford, CEO of Compassion, provided the answer. The opposite of poverty is "enough."

Enough to eat that you don't have malnutrition. Enough health care that you don't have parasites in your stomach. Enough money that you can provide a roof over your family's head, basic nutrition, and health care.

Most of us live in a place that has "more than enough," and quite honestly that makes us wealthy. I've never considered myself wealthy in forty-plus years of life. I grew up in a family that was comfortable. We would have never been considered wealthy by cultural standards—but we were. Mark and I have scrimped, penny pinched, and done without in many areas of our life. There have been many times that we've wondered if we'll make it financially. But we've always had enough . . . in fact we've had more than enough. I just didn't realize it because I've never seen someone who really didn't have enough.

There was a time when Jesus was faced with not having enough. He stood face-to-face with over five thousand people who had listened to Him teach for several days. On the third day, Jesus told the disciples to feed the crowd. The disciples replied that they couldn't feed the crowd because they only had five loaves of bread and two fish. Jesus took that meager offering, blessed it, and multiplied it miraculously to feed the men, women, and children. After everyone's bellies were full, the disciples picked up twelve basketfuls of leftovers! (You can read this story in Matthew 14:13–21.)

Sometimes I've felt like there isn't enough time, money, or me to go around. But there is. I just need a little bit of perspective to see the picture accurately. And sometimes I believe that's the miracle that God does in my life. He helps me see things differently so I can process life more accurately or be creative with what I have.

There are also times when Jesus asks for my five loaves and two fish so He can do His own miracle. Our family sponsors a child in

Honduras through Compassion. Yes it's a stretch for us financially some months but God works a miracle in that child's life with our meager offering of $38 a month. He accomplishes hundreds of dollars of benefits (food, medical care, tutoring, and more) with that $38 of "loaves and fish" each month.

Most of us have to work with limited resources of time, money, and energy. But what I've learned is that God will give us exactly what we need exactly when we need it. If He needs to work a miracle to make that happen, He will. If He needs to change our perspective to make that happen, He'll do that, as well.

Pray . . .

Jesus, You have given me enough time,
money, and energy. In fact, I've never understood
just how wealthy I am. Help me to be a good steward
of what You've given me. And help me walk by faith,
trusting You to provide exactly what I need
exactly when I need it.

Discover . . .

Read Matthew chapters 24 and 25.
Thank God for the Bible and how it guides our life.

TRUTH . . .

Your word is a lamp to my feet
and a light for my path.

PSALM 119:105

CHAPTER 12

DISCOVER GOD'S TRUTH:
JESUS TRUSTED

The Truth about Faith

nne, I need to talk with you." I began the dreaded conversation with our almost sixteen-year-old daughter one Saturday morning. "You know that dad and I were saving money to buy a third car for the family so that when you turn sixteen you'd have a vehicle to use. What we didn't count on was our well running dry (oh the joys of living in the country!). When we had to have a new well dug we had to use the car money. Now we won't be able to purchase a car."

Anne's face reflected her disappointment. I was disappointed too. With four children (only God knew then that we would adopt a fifth child just two years later!) I was looking forward to some help with the taxi responsibilities. "I'm bummed, Mom, but I understand. I guess I'll just have to pray for a car."

I affirmed her decision to pray, but I had no idea how serious she was. Several weeks after our conversation Anne popped in the kitchen while I was making dinner and said, "Mom, you know how I told you that I would pray for a car? I just wanted you to know that I am praying specifically like you've taught me. I'm praying that it would have an automatic transmission because I don't know how to drive a stick shift. I'm also praying that it would be a four-door since I'll be taking my brothers and sisters so many places and it's a pain to climb in and out of the backseat of a two-door. And I decided to ask God if it would be possible for it to be blue because it's my favorite color."

I stared at her in astonishment. "Wow! That's a tall order," I responded. "I think if God provides you a car, you'd better be ready to take it as it is even if it means learning to drive a stick, climbing out of the backseat, or learning to like another color!"

"I know, Mom," she replied, "but God tells us to ask specifically so I am. And I believe He can provide it if it's in His will."

I was astonished at my daughter's spiritual maturity, but my heart was torn in two directions. I was so proud of my daughter's faith. She was taking God at His word and her belief was strong. At the same time I desperately wanted to protect my girl from disappointment. This was a tall order and even though I believed that God *could* provide, I just didn't know that He really *would*, and I didn't want her to get hurt.

Several days after that conversation, I stumbled out of bed early one morning and decided to check e-mail before everyone woke up and the morning chaos began. I noticed an e-mail from a man at our church who had never sent e-mail to us before. When I opened his message and read it, tears started rolling down my cheeks:

Hello Mark and Jill,

I'm in the process of purchasing a new car and my old one still runs fine but it isn't worth a whole lot. I've been praying about what to do with the old car and today, as I was walking down the hall at work, God brought you to my mind. I think you have a daughter who will be driving soon and I'm wondering if you would like a car for her. Here are the basic details: it's a 1983 Honda Accord, automatic transmission, four doors. Don't know that it matters, but it's blue. Let me know if you'd be interested. If you are, I'm willing to give it to your family.

Mike

"Yes, Mike," I whispered aloud, "it does matter that it's blue. It matters a lot!" I couldn't believe my eyes. I was humbled by my daughter's faith and God's miraculous provision. God's truth came to my mind, "According to your faith will it be done to you" (Matthew 9:29).

If you don't think that God performs miracles today, then think again.

A Front Row Seat at Watching God Work

Jesus worked many miracles during His time on this earth. He had the ability to do so because He was God in the flesh. The books of the Bible known as the gospels, Matthew, Mark, Luke, and John record over forty different miracles that Jesus performed. Sometimes He cured a sickness or disability such as healing the woman who had been bleeding for twelve years (Matthew 9:20–22). Sometimes His miracles showed power over death such as the time that He called Jairus's daughter back to life after she had died (Matthew 9:18–26).

Other miraculous deeds had to do with changing nature such as the time He walked on water (John 6:16–21), He miraculously showed His power over the spirit world when He drove the demon out of the mute man (Matthew 9:32–33).

Of course we see the miracle of life over death in Jesus' own life when He rose from the dead three days after He was crucified on the cross (1 Corinthians 15:3–4).

Reading about His miracles deepens our belief and increases our faith. When Jesus healed, changed nature, or brought someone back to life people were able to witness God at work. Today you and I are also able to see God at work! Every time I've trusted God, He's never failed me. When I've let Him lead or trusted Him to provide, He's always done so—maybe not in the way I expected—but He's always responded in some way. I like to say that it's like having a front-row seat at watching God work!

Our Bread-and-Milk God Story

Mark had been working for some time at a new nonprofit ministry when his boss came to him with a dilemma. "Mark, we've lost the private funding we've had for your salary. The donor's investments went bad and they need a few months to recover. We believe we'll be able to reinstate your salary in three months with back pay, but until then we can't pay you. If you need to seek out another job, we understand. But if you can stick with us, we'd love to have you stay on."

That was quite a request to make of a man with a large family to feed. Mark came home and we talked about the situation. We agreed to pray about it individually for several days before making a decision. When we came back together several days later we discovered that both of us were hearing God say, *Trust Me*. We felt that we weren't to change anything. It was a scary thought, yet we both had an unusual peace about it (and no, we didn't have three months' worth of salary in the bank like they say you are supposed to have!).

I immediately got busy doing what I could. I called our utility companies and creditors and made whatever arrangements I could for delayed or smaller payments for a limited time. I looked at what little money we had in our savings and divided it up to pay the bills we would need to pay. I then took an inventory of the food in our pantry and two freezers, writing down everything we had in the house to eat including the two cans of beets I didn't know I even had that had been pushed to the back of the pantry shelf! Our family doesn't eat beets (well, not until we adopted Kolya years later from Russia—beets are a staple in Russia and Kolya loves them. I now buy them regularly!), so I didn't know why I had them. I sat down and laid out a possible meal plan for twelve weeks. When Mark came home from work that afternoon, I shared the results of my planning with him. "I've made arrangements for the monthly bills and I have figured out a way that we can eat without having to go to the grocery store. The only thing we won't have are the fresh foods like bread and milk, but we can trust God for that."

The only thing we won't have are the fresh foods like bread and milk, but we can trust God for that.

Honestly, in my mind, I thought that maybe God would send a music opportunity my way—sometimes I sing or play for weddings and earn fifty dollars or so. Mark also laid carpet on the side and I thought maybe God would send him a small carpet job each month that would pay enough for us to go to the grocery store to get bread, milk, and maybe fresh fruit and vegetables. But God's ways are not our ways and God had another plan in mind.

We shared with our children that we were in a season of trusting God. No new clothes, no convenience snack food in the snack drawer, no extra money to go out for ice cream. We reassured them that we would be okay, but that we all had to respect the sacrifices, and we needed to thank God for His creative provisions already. At every meal we sat down and held hands to pray, thanking God for how He had already provided and making our simple request for bread and milk.

A couple of weeks after we started our faith journey, I received a call from my neighbor Orville. We live in the country so neighbors aren't "over the fence" type of neighbors. Rather they live "down the road" and we don't often interact with one another. Orville farmed all the land around our home so he'd stop by and chat during planting season or while harvesting, but other than that we didn't see each another a whole lot.

When I picked up the phone Orville said, "Jill, do you need some bread?"

I was caught off guard by the absence of small talk you often have at the start of a phone conversation and by the nature of his question. "Well, Orville, actually yes, we do need some bread," I responded almost with a question in my voice.

"Okay, I'll be by in a few minutes," he continued. "I've got some you can have." I hung up the phone thinking that that was the oddest phone conversation I'd ever had.

Within minutes Orville's truck pulled into our driveway. As I walked out to meet him I noticed the bed of his truck was piled high . . . with bread! As Orville parked and got out of the truck, I teasingly said, "Orville, what did you do? Did you rob a bread store?"

"Oh no," he responded, "I have an agreement with a couple of grocery stores to haul away their expired bread products. I then take it out of its wrappings and feed it to my cows. Honestly, there's always more than I can use, and we're really not supposed to eat it, but much of it is still good, so Betty and I always pull out some before I head out to the barn. Today as I was driving home I suddenly thought 'Those Savages have a lot of kids. Maybe they'd like some of this bread,' so I called you."

I stood there amazed with tears in my eyes. When I was finally able to pull myself together to get a few words out, I said, "Orville, are you aware of what is going on with our family?" His puzzled look indicated he didn't and he replied that he didn't know what I was talking about. I briefly filled him in on Mark's situation with not being paid at work and I finished with, "So every evening when we sit down together as a family we thank God for what He's provided and we pray for bread and milk."

Orville's eyes lit up. "You need milk?" he asked. Before I could respond he opened the cab of his truck to reveal about twelve gallons of milk. "These expired yesterday but if you freeze them they'll be just fine," he declared.

I couldn't hold it together anymore. I stood there looking at that bread and milk that had been delivered in the most unlikely form and I praised God in my heart for His incredible provision.

Orville offered to carry the milk into my kitchen while I dug through the bed of his truck to find whatever bread I wanted. As I began to look I was amazed at the selection—there was every kind of bread product available: English muffins, donuts, bagels, wheat bread, white bread, raisin bread, and rainbow bread (I hadn't even known rainbow bread existed!). Most of these were name brand, what I would consider expensive, breads that we'd never eaten before! I filled several grocery sacks with the bread I knew our family would eat. Orville helped me carry it all in the house and then we took a few minutes to pour off a little bit of milk from each gallon into a pitcher so I could freeze the plastic jugs since the milk would expand when it froze.

I gave Orville a big hug. I thanked him for his gift and said, "Orville, I want you to know that today God spoke to you. You didn't just think that the Savage family might need this food; God prompted you, and you listened and responded. Thank you for allowing God to lead you and for blessing our family."

I was home alone when Orville came that day. Mark was at work and the kids were at school. You can imagine their surprise when they arrived home and I was able to tell them what God did that day! As we gathered around the table that evening, we thanked God for His incredible provisions and we didn't ask for a single thing!

Our Adoption God Story

Several years after the bread-and-milk experience, God allowed us to walk by faith again. At the end of January 2003, I spoke at a moms group near my home. In addition to my keynote message, there were also four workshops being offered for the moms to attend. I first thought I'd sit in on the adoption workshop and then I reconsidered and decided that I didn't want to open that door. I chose instead to attend the workshop on parenting teenagers. After the group disbanded for the morning, I began packing away my resources. A friend, Cathy, who had attended the adoption workshop walked up to me and said, "Jill, you are pretty networked. Do you know any family who might be interested in adopting an eight-year-old little boy from Russia whose best friend is a little girl named Nadia who was adopted by a family here in Bloomington just eighteen months ago?" She said it all so quickly without taking a breath.

"No," I responded slowly. "I don't know of anyone interested in adopting an eight-year-old."

"Well just in case you think of someone," she continued, "here's his picture and a contact number for more information."

I glanced down at the picture she handed me and caught my breath. This little blond-headed guy looked just like my boys.

He looked like he belonged in *our* family. Then immediately God gently whispered to my heart, *Oh Jill, let Me introduce you to your new son!* A lump formed in my throat and I quickly told my friend to please put the picture away. She asked about my emotional response and I told her that I couldn't explain it but that I didn't want to talk about it anymore. She told me that if I was that moved by it, maybe I ought to put it in my Bible and pray about it. I teasingly told her that I thought she should just go home. Cathy tucked the picture away amidst my resources and I found it again later in the afternoon. When Mark came home unexpectedly early, I hesitantly shared with him most of my experience earlier in the day. I say "most" because I couldn't bring myself to tell him that God had told me this little boy was ours—I still couldn't believe that I actually heard that! What I said instead was, "My heart is tugged by this little boy's picture. I think we need to be praying for this boy because I think we must know the family who is supposed to adopt him." Okay, it wasn't the whole truth . . . but the whole truth sounded absolutely crazy!

Mark asked to see the picture. I showed it to him and he became very quiet. "Jill," he whispered, "this little guy looks like he belongs in *our* family."

"Don't say that!" I declared too loudly. Now I had to tell him the rest of the story—how God had seemingly tapped me on the shoulder and introduced me to our new son. We both stood in the dining room not exactly knowing what to say or do. This was an insane thought. We've never talked about adopting. We've never even *thought* about adopting. We decided that all we could do right now was pray. And we did.

After a short period of time, both of us were still sensing God was calling us to make Kolya a part of our family. We decided to discuss the possibility with our children. Unsure of the response we would get, we were thrilled when all four of them responded very positively. You see, up to this point God had even been preparing their hearts, but we just hadn't seen it. Our oldest, Anne, had consistently communicated to us that she didn't think our family was complete. She'd mentioned it once or twice a year for several years, but we dismissed her comments with an assurance that we were done having children. Our youngest, Austin, had inherited bunk beds two months before this picture was placed in my hand. Each night when we tucked him in his new bed he would ask, "Who's going to sleep in that other bed?" We'd answer that no one was going to sleep in it regularly—it would be used when his cousins spent the night or when he had a friend overnight. He'd respond with, "No, someone's gotta sleep in that bed!" We went through this routine each night and honestly, it was getting a little old. When we shared with the kids about the possibility of having a new brother, Anne's response was, "I told you our family wasn't complete!" And Austin said, "That's who's supposed to sleep in my bunk bed!" After this, we knew, without a doubt, that Kolya was to be a part of our family. We prayed together as a family about this opportunity and continued praying over the next week. The unity and excitement continued to grow.

We officially began the adoption process in February. In April, our home study was completed and Mark and I made our first of two trips to Russia. Nadia's family was thrilled as their dream of finding a home for Kolya was coming true. We later found out that the Cavanagh family had adopted Nadia when she was six. She and Kolya had been in the orphanage together their entire lives. From the time Nadia began to speak English she would tell her mom and dad, "We have to find a momma and a papa for my friend Kolya."

Our first trip was a lesson of culture for Mark and me. Kolya was unsure of this mama and papa thing but warmed up to us in time. He spoke not one word of English and we spoke about ten words of Russian. But we found that charades works well to communicate just about anything and we were on our way to making the connection with him.

I struggled as a mom on that first trip. I didn't feel instant love for this child. I knew he was to be a part of our family and I knew that love would come, but I desperately wanted to bond with him. When we made a call to our kids back in the States and Austin cried for me to come home, I lost it. I poured out my heart to God and asked Him to help me make the connection. On our last day together, it happened. When Kolya began to understand that we would have to leave and then return to get him, he cried and cried and cried. They were the first tears we'd seen him shed. And God began to allow the bonding to happen as I comforted him, wiped his tears and whispered "loo blu," which is "I love you" in Russian. This was indeed my child and he needed me as much as my four at home needed me.

We completed the adoption with a second trip at the end of August, bringing Kolya home on September 3. Kolya and his best friend, Nadia, were reunited on September 5, 2003.

Our biggest challenge of this faith journey was the financial piece of the picture. We said yes before we understood that adopting from Russia is one of the most expensive international adoption experiences. In February, I had lunch with a friend and shared with her both the excitement and the fears I was experiencing. Financially, this just didn't make sense for our family. Our oldest daughter was starting college in the fall and we had less than $500 in our savings account—not exactly a down payment on what would be a $34,000 adoption. My friend Julie listened to me fret and then she said, "Jill, our God owns the cattle on a thousand hills. He just needs to sell a few cows to make this happen." Wow! What a perspective that was. Indeed, over the next nine months we witnessed the sale of those cows, one gift at a time! Here's what God did:

- Our family pulled together and created a fund-raising project that brought in over $2000.

- Our oldest daughter, Anne, created her own fund-raiser she called "Cooking for Kolya" where she made an order form of freezer meals and sold them to her teachers at school. Word spread about her little business in no time. Soon she had made more than $1,000.

- We received $5,000 in donations from friends and family.

- We received a matching grant of $5,000 from Life International (now known as Lifesong). God was selling more cows.

- We were awarded a $2,000 grant from Shaohanna's Hope. Thank you God!

- We received another $2,000 from a family friend.

- I received an unexpected check from book sales for $2,000. Go God!

Each time God sold cows we thanked Him for His faithfulness. However, it was God's final provision that absolutely astonished us. I had written an article on creative ways to finance adoption that was printed in the fall 2003 edition of *Money Matters* magazine.

Within a few days of the article's printing, I received an e-mail from a man in Alabama. He and his wife had read the article and found it very encouraging. They had also adopted just two years earlier. He shared about their adoption and then asked, "Have you and your husband completely paid for your adoption?"

I was a little uncomfortable writing him back and saying that while God had provided in so many ways, indeed we still had $15,000 of expenses we were paying on. He asked for a phone call and we had a nice chat. He then indicated that he and his wife felt led to help us in some way. He would pray over the weekend and let us know. We didn't hear from him for several weeks, but then an envelope came in the mail. In it was one check for $15,000 and a note that said, "Please tell your family that a bunch of old country folks in Alabama send Christ's love." Wow. *God sold a whole herd of cows that day!*

We saw Him work in ways we never could have imagined and our faith, as well as the faith of others who witnessed the miracles, grew exponentially.

Indeed this was a journey of faith for our family. It made no sense, but God's ways are not our ways. He is our great Provider. We saw Him work in ways we never could have imagined and our faith, as well as the faith of others who witnessed the miracles, grew exponentially.

Turn Fear into Faith

Hearing stories of God's adequacy in the midst of our inadequacy does the same thing for us that seeing God work firsthand did for the disciples who lived with Jesus. Can you imagine their conversations when they saw someone who had been dead come to life? How about when they witnessed Jesus feed five thousand people with just a small amount of bread and fish? And then there was the time Jesus walked on the water. Let's take a look at that specific situation to see what we can learn about walking by faith.

As soon as the meal was finished, [Jesus] insisted that the disciples get in the boat and go on ahead to the other side while he dismissed the people. With the crowd dispersed, he climbed the mountain so he could be by himself and pray. He stayed there alone, late into the night.

Meanwhile, the boat was far out to sea when the wind came up against them and they were battered by the waves. At about four o'clock in the morning, Jesus came toward them walking on the water. They were scared out of their wits. "A ghost!" they said, crying out in terror.

But Jesus was quick to comfort them. "Courage, it's me. Don't be afraid."

Peter, suddenly bold, said, "Master, if it's really you, call me to come to you on the water."

He said, "Come ahead."

Jumping out of the boat, Peter walked on the water to Jesus. But when he looked down at the waves churning beneath his feet, he lost his nerve and started to sink. He cried, "Master, save me!"

Jesus didn't hesitate. He reached down and grabbed his hand. Then he said, "Faint-heart, what got into you?"

The two of them climbed into the boat, and the wind died down. The disciples in the boat, having watched the whole thing, worshiped Jesus, saying, "This is it! You are God's Son for sure!" (Matthew 14:22–32 THE MESSAGE)

I love this story because I believe it gives us some important steps to take to turn fear into faith. Let's take a look at the lessons we can draw from this story.

1. Obey fully—Jesus insisted the disciples get in the boat and head out without Him. They didn't necessarily understand why, but they did as He said. When God asks us to walk by faith we don't always understand the plan, but we can learn to trust that God does have a plan.

2. Accept God's comfort—Jesus comforted the disciples when they were afraid of the unknown. Walking by faith sometimes requires us to do something we've never done before. Sometimes the light is only shining on the next step and we can't see the big picture. God's Word and His peace provide comfort in the midst of obedience.

3. Keep a childlike faith—I love Peter's childlike faith. He often speaks before he thinks about what he is doing. Many times we rationalize ourselves right out of obedience because we think too hard about the logic of what God is asking. Children are rarely logical in their thinking. And God is rarely logical—His ways are not our ways!

4. Listen for God's invitation—Peter didn't just jump out of the boat, he had a conversation with the Lord that prompted the invitation to come. Stepping out in faith outside of God's will is foolishness. When we hear God's direction and it is congruent with God's truth and confirmed by believers around us, then we need to get out of the boat.

5. Get out of the boat—Peter got out of the boat but the other eleven disciples stayed in the safety of the boat. They didn't even inquire of Jesus if they could walk to Him on the water. When we stay in the boat we miss the blessing of experiencing God at work firsthand. When we get out of the boat of our comfort zone and step into the water of faith, we experience blessings that only come when taking steps of faith.

6. Keep focused on Jesus—Peter stepped out of the boat and began to walk toward Jesus, but the minute he took his eyes off Jesus and began to look at the waves around him, he began to sink. Too often we look at the mountains instead of the Mountain Mover and that's when we begin to doubt. We have to keep our eyes on God, trusting His ways. Proverbs 3:5 tells us, "Trust in the Lord with all your heart and lean not on your own understanding." When Peter looked down at the waves he couldn't understand how he was actually walking on the water. Trying to understand from a human perspective caused him to lose faith.

7. Grab God's hand—While God may not physically extend His hand to us like Jesus was able to do for Peter, He still sends help in our unbelief. Sometimes that hand is a reminder of God's truth (in the Bible), sometimes it's the help or encouragement from a friend. When my friend Julie shared with me about God's cattle on a thousand hills (from Psalm 50:10) during our adoption process, God used her to extend His hand to me. I was starting to waver, looking at the waves rather than Jesus. Julie's encouragement allowed me to grab God's hand and focus on Him once again.

8. Recognize the value of storms in our lives   Just as our muscles get strong only when they meet resistance, so our faith only grows when it is battling a storm. Don't run from storms. Run to God instead. It is the storms of our life that bring us into the deepest intimacy with God.

9. Respond with worship—When God works in our lives, we need to respond by giving Him the credit. Thanking God, giving Him praise for being faithful, and telling of His work in our lives are all ways that we give God the glory He deserves.

I Can't but God Can

"Now faith is being sure of what we hope for and certain of what we do not see." Those words from Hebrews 11:1 are an accurate description of what faith is. God wants us to learn to trust Him more every day and trusting in someone we can't see is a stretch for most of us. But the more intimate we become with God, the more we can learn to discern His voice, then the more we can trust Him.

Now faith is being sure of what we hope for and certain of what we do not see.

The Bible is filled with "I Can't but God Can" stories. Hebrews 11 is one of my favorite chapters in the Bible because it summarizes so many of the stories of ordinary people who let God do extraordinary things in their lives. Here's a brief overview of some of the faith stories mentioned in the chapter:

By faith we understand that the universe was formed at God's command, so that what is seen was not made out of what was visible. (verse 3)

By faith Enoch was taken from this life, so that he did not experience death; he could not be found, because God had taken him away. (verse 5)

By faith Noah, when warned about things not yet seen, in holy fear built an ark to save his family. (verse 7)

By faith Abraham, when called to go to a place he would later receive as his inheritance, obeyed and went, even though he did not know where he was going. (verse 8)

By faith Abraham, even though he was past age—and Sarah herself was barren—was enabled to become a father because he considered him faithful who had made the promise. (verse 11)

By faith Abraham, when God tested him, offered Isaac as a sacrifice. He who had received the promises was about to sacrifice his one and only son, even though God had said to him, "It is through Isaac that your offspring will be reckoned." Abraham reasoned that God could raise the dead, and figuratively speaking, he did receive Isaac back from death. (verses 17–19)

By faith Moses' parents hid him for three months after he was born, because they saw he was no ordinary child, and they were not afraid of the king's edict. (verse 23)

By faith Moses, when he had grown up, refused to be known as the son of Pharaoh's daughter. He chose to be mistreated along with the people of God rather than to enjoy the pleasures of sin for a short time. He regarded disgrace for the sake of Christ as of greater value than the treasures of Egypt, because he was looking ahead to his reward. (verses 24–26)

By faith the people passed through the Red Sea as on dry land; but when the Egyptians tried to do so, they were drowned (verse 29)

By faith the walls of Jericho fell, after the people had marched around them for seven days. (verse 30)

By faith the prostitute Rahab, because she welcomed the spies, was not killed with those who were disobedient. (verse 31)

And what more shall I say? I do not have time to tell about Gideon, Barak, Samson, Jephthah, David, Samuel and the prophets, who through faith conquered kingdoms, administered justice, and gained what was promised; who shut the mouths of lions, quenched the fury of the flames, and escaped the edge of the sword; whose weakness was turned to strength; and who became powerful in battle and routed foreign armies. (verse 32–34)

Each of these stories tells of God's power and what happens when someone like you or me chooses to look at God's abilities rather than our inabilities. And that is the essence of faith.

It's important to understand, too, that while God always takes care of us, He doesn't always choose to do so in miraculous ways. Sometimes His ways are more logical and practical. Several years ago our family went through a difficult financial season. With unexpected medical bills and rising fuel prices we had more outgo than income. My prayers seemed to be unanswered as I attempted to move money around from month to month to make ends meet. I had faith God would provide, but it seemed He was taking a long time. One Sunday our church announced that they were going to be offering a Christian money management class called *Financial Peace.*[19] I knew that was God's answer to my prayer. Mark and I took the class, changed the way we managed our money, and slowly worked our way out of our crisis. There was no money dropped from heaven, no unexpected checks, but God still provided—this time with an educational opportunity that gave us the wisdom and direction we needed.

Jesus had faith in His Father; He performed miracles by faith and taught about faith. As we grow to know Jesus more intimately, let's walk by faith, trusting God's ways and not our own. Let's live our lives with the mind-set that "I can't, but God can!"

Jesus, Thank You for living a life that showed Your supernatural power. Too often I look down at the waves instead of up at You. Help me keep my eyes on You and only You. I want to believe more fully and walk by faith. Thank You for being both trustworthy and faithful. Show me how to turn my fears into faith, loving You more deeply along the way.

19. www.daveramsey.com.

Perspective

I need a break!

J'm a terrible mother!" cried the voice as soon as I picked up the phone and said hello. I had no idea who this desperate woman was who had called my number. Before I could respond, she continued crying and talking. I could only understand every third or fourth word, but I finally made out the names "Caleb" and "Conner" and realized this was my sister!

"Juli," I spoke soothingly, "you're not a terrible mother. You need a break. This is when you need to give yourself a time-out so you gather yourself together."

"I know," she sobbed. "I'm sitting out in the garage talking to you!"

Every mom has had a moment like that. Either we lose it with tears or we lose it with anger. But losing it is reactive to life, and what you and I have to learn to do is to be proactive in taking care of ourselves so we'll be better equipped to take care of our families.

Jesus was a master at this. He carried the weight of the world on His shoulders. He was in high demand. He was followed, touched, begged, invited, questioned, and criticized each and every day. But Jesus knew that in order to be available to the world He had to spend time with the Father. Remember what we've read in Mark 1:35: "Very early in the morning, while it was still dark, Jesus got up, left the house and went off to a solitary place, where he prayed." Jesus looked at what was ahead of Him and He prepared Himself for it. You and I need to do the same.

I love this verse in Luke: "At daybreak Jesus went out to a solitary place. The people were looking for him and when they came to where he was, they tried to keep him from leaving them" (4:42).

As we read on, the passage explains that Jesus must leave to preach to people in other places. However, doesn't the first part sound like a mom's life? Mom had gone to be alone for a while; the children looked for her and when they found her they tried to keep her from going off to be alone again!

When Austin was little his "l's" sounded like "w's." He also was very clingy so if I went anywhere he would whine and cry, "Mommmmmmmy . . . don't weave meeeeeeee." What Austin didn't understand, though, is that I was a better mommy if I left occasionally. Taking care of myself isn't a selfish act. In fact, doing so is what allows me to expand my ability to serve.

The first step in taking care of ourselves is spending time with God. Practicing the presence of God and talking to Him throughout the day is one way of doing that. Following Jesus' example of getting up a little early or having some time at night where we keep an appointment with God is valuable, as well. When you and I do this it fills up our spiritual fuel tank, which keeps us running on full instead of sputtering along on empty.

Self-care also happens when there's balance in our life. Jesus took time to visit with friends, attend weddings, and share meals with people. You and I need to balance our lives. If we're home all day with small children we need some adult time. If we have a lot on the schedule, we also need time to rest and relax. We have to have a balance between taking care of our children and taking care of our marriage.

And finally, self-care happens when we are in tune with ourselves. You are unique. What specifically do you need? What fuels you emotionally? Reading a book? Exercising? Talking with a friend? Once you can identify the type of fuel you need, schedule those activities on the calendar. It's not selfish at all . . . it's wise.

Jesus was intentional about finding time to refuel. He knew there were many demands upon His time and energy and that He had to be a good steward of His body, soul, and mind. Nobody had to tell Him, "Jesus, go rest." Instead He recognized His need to pull away from the crowds and find the refreshment He needed.

As moms, we need to do the same. People and responsibilities demand much from us and we have to be good stewards of our body, soul, and mind. We can't wait until we're drained dry or until someone comes along and offers to watch our kids (like that happens very often!). Instead we have to learn to be proactive about our self-care so that we can be ready to meet the needs of our family.

Pray . . .

*Jesus, Thank You for showing me the importance of
pulling away from the crowds and finding time to refuel.
Help me to become reacquainted with myself to allow me
to know what it is that I need. And then give me the courage
to make it happen. No one gave You a break . . .*

REAL MOMS . . . REAL JESUS

*You recognized the need and took
one every day with God. Help me do the same.*

Discover . . .

*Read Matthew chapters 26, 27, and 28.
Ask God to give you a fresh understanding of Jesus'
death on the cross and what that means for you personally.*

TRUTH . . .

You are my friends when you do the things I
command you. I'm no longer calling you servants
because servants don't understand what their master
is thinking and planning. No, I've named you friends
because I've let you in on everything
I've heard from the Father.

JOHN 15:14–15 (THE MESSAGE)

CHAPTER 13

DISCOVER GOD'S TRUTH:
JESUS LET GO

The Truth about Surrendering

The young man sitting across from Mark and me in the restaurant was sweating profusely despite the cool temperature in the restaurant. He was obviously nervous and seemed to be talking in circles about his relationship with our daughter Anne, but not quite able to get out the question he wanted to ask. Finally, Mark took pity upon this poor soul and asked, "Matt, are you trying to ask us if you can marry Anne?" "Yes sir, I am," he quickly replied.

My heart was immediately tugged in a million different directions and my mind jumped from one thought to another: *I'm not ready to let go yet. I don't know if I can do this. Is this the young man I've been praying for for the past twenty years? She's dated with integrity . . . I'm so proud of her. How much time do I have left before I have to let go? I've really been letting go since day one, haven't I, God? We've never been here, Lord, what do we say?*

After a brief discussion we gave Matt and Anne our blessing. Wedding plans soon followed and I began the final parenting step of letting go.

The Art of Letting Go

Mothering could be likened to painting a picture. From the time your child is born you are partnering with God in painting a picture of her life. A brush stroke of encouragement added, a shade of talent developed, a line of discipline drawn . . . each and every day we are adding to the picture of who she is. There comes a time, however, when the brush that is painting the canvas of their life must be transferred from your hand to hers. That's when we have to let go and let God. But even this experience is not unfamiliar to God.

To fully comprehend this we need to understand that there is one God, but He consists of three distinct persons: Father, Son, and Holy Spirit. This is known as the Trinity; each person in the Trinity is God. God the Father sent Himself, in the form of His Son, Jesus Christ, to earth ultimately giving God the human experience that we've been building upon in this book. Because of this, we have a God who understands our human experiences because they were His as well. The Holy Spirit lives inside every Christian, guiding him or her to live according to God's ways.

Understanding that, let's get back to God's experience of letting go. God sent His Son, Jesus, to live on this earth. He let Him leave heaven, watched Him experience the challenges of human life, and saw Him suffer at the hands of the very people He created.

What marvels me about God is that He doesn't ask us to do anything He wasn't willing to do Himself. He led the way for us in every step of this journey of life. He painted a picture of letting go that we can refer to as we're painting our own pictures throughout life. The truth is, however, that we will be able to let go as a parent more easily if we've learned to "let go and let God" in our own personal life.

Who's in the Driver's Seat?

Sitting in the front passenger seat of our minivan, my right foot kept looking for the brake that didn't exist. My soon-to-be sixteen-year-old was doing her best, but the inexperience was evident. This felt like the ultimate act of letting go and putting my life in God's hands!

Thus far, we've put three teenagers through driver's training, and each time I'm reminded of how that experience is an analogy to our life with God. God wants to drive, but we have to be willing to move to the passenger seat. That's a hard thing for "control freak" people (like many moms are!) to do. This analogy brings up a question that demands an answer: Who's in the driver's seat of my life?

When I was nineteen years old, I accepted Jesus Christ as my Savior. It was several years later before I understood what it meant for Him to be Lord of my life. In other words, when I said yes to God, I experienced forgiveness and grace but I didn't understand that God had an abundant life waiting for me if I would just learn to let Him lead. When I finally moved from the driver's seat to the passenger seat and let God take His place at the steering wheel of my life, I began to experience a new intimacy with Christ and a deeper faith than I could have ever imagined. That experience of letting God be Lord is called submission.

To submit is to yield to the leadership or authority of someone else. Submission recognizes that life isn't all about us and it recognizes that God can see the bigger picture of our lives. Because of His ability to see the big picture, we can trust His direction for our lives.

Think of it from a parenting perspective. Would you or I intentionally lead our child down a wrong path? Would we tell our child they can't do something without a good reason? Would we knowingly say yes to something that would cause them harm? You and I lead and guide our children because of the big picture we see for their lives. We have experience and a perspective that gives us wisdom to help steer their lives in the right direction. We won't do it perfectly, but our children will be better off with our guidance than left to make their own uneducated and undirected decisions.

God can see the bigger picture of our lives. Because of His ability to see the big picture, we can trust His direction for our lives.

When thinking about this for my own life I sometimes picture a parade in my mind. I look at the parade from two different perspectives. The first perspective is as a parade participant. Four years in marching band have honed this picture in my mind. As a participant in a parade, you can only see what's happening directly in front of you. Your view is extremely limited. The second perspective is as a parade viewer in a tall building. I've had several experiences of watching a parade from a high-rise building and it's amazing how you not only see what's right below you, you can also see the beginning and ending of the parade. Your view is expanded greatly, allowing you to see things the parade participants will never be able to see.

You and I have an earthly perspective. We are participants in the parade of life. God has a heavenly perspective. He can see the big picture from the beginning to the end of time. Because of that, we can trust Him to lead and guide us, understanding He can see things we are unable to see.

The core of submission is recognizing that someone has a better perspective than we have and trusting that they are better equipped to make decisions because of that perspective. Do you believe that for your life? Do you believe that God can see the big picture and that that actually makes Him better equipped than you are to sit in the driver's seat? I hope that after you come to know Jesus better, you will find yourself closer to being able to move aside and let God lead. It's the hardest "flesh" versus "spirit" battle we'll ever face. Our flesh wants to maintain control when the Spirit says, "Let go."

It's Your Gig, God

We see the ultimate act of submission in Jesus' life in His journey to the cross. Knowing what He was facing, He struggled with the task before Him. The first time we see this is in the garden of Gethsemane, just days before the crucifixion.

> Then Jesus went with them to the olive grove called Gethsemane, and he said, "Sit here while I go over there to pray." He took Peter and Zebedee's two sons, James and John, and he became anguished and distressed. He told them, "My soul is crushed with grief to the point of death. Stay here and keep watch with me."

> He went on a little farther and bowed with his face to the ground, praying, "My Father! If it is possible, let this cup of suffering be taken away from me. Yet I want your will to be done, not mine."

Then he returned to the disciples and found them asleep. He said to Peter, "Couldn't you watch with me even one hour? Keep watch and pray, so that you will not give in to temptation. For the spirit is willing, but the body is weak!"

Then Jesus left them a second time and prayed, "My Father! If this cup cannot be taken away unless I drink it, your will be done." (Matthew 26:36–42 NLT)

Can you feel His agony? Can you sense the struggle? Jesus was battling the two perspectives and because of His dual nature, He could equally see them both. The fully human Jesus who was a participant in the parade of life could see the painful death He knew was imminent. The fully God Jesus could see the big picture of the sacrifice He was about to make that would change God's relationship with His people for the rest of eternity. Do you see how we have a God who understands our struggle to submit? He's talked the talk and walked the walk. And He's not asking us to do anything He wasn't willing to do Himself.

As we look more carefully at Jesus' time in the garden of Gethsemane, I believe we can find wisdom for our walk toward submission.

1. Don't go it alone—Once they arrived at the garden, Jesus asked the disciples to stay in the general vicinity of the garden. He then asked Peter, James, and John to come with Him as He went to find a place to pray. He told them what He was feeling and asked them to actively engage in His agony.

2. Get honest with God—God knew what Jesus was feeling and He knows what we are feeling, too. Getting honest with God expresses our emotions and admits our fears. Until we can

get honest and in tune with our flesh, we won't be able to actively engage the spirit.

3. Seek God's will—Look to God's Word and listen to the Holy Spirit to discern God's will. This begins the process of letting go of our agenda and letting God lead.

4. Ask others to pray—Jesus could have done this whole thing alone, but He didn't. He chose to invite the imperfect disciples into His inner circle. We're not designed to do life alone. We need others to pray with us when we are going through a tough time. Even though they may not do that perfectly, their presence is still important.

5. Recognize the battle—Jesus says "the spirit is willing, but the body is weak." He knows the battle He is facing is a spiritual one. He understands the temptation to walk in the flesh and that the only way to fight that battle is with prayer and God's truth.

6. Submit to God's direction—After He vocalized His struggle and fought the accompanying spiritual battle, we see Jesus submit with the words, "Your will be done." This is where we might say, "It's Your gig, God. I'm going to let You lead and trust You fully."

Shortly after He voiced that prayer, He was arrested. His arrest and trial signaled the beginning of the end of His human experience. His ultimate act of submission is found in His final words as He hung on the cross paying for your sins and mine. "Jesus called loudly, 'Father, I place my life in your hands!' Then he breathed his last" (Luke 23:46 MSG).

Oh, how God must long to hear us utter these words: "Father, I place my life in your hands." He wants us to get out of the way and let Him do his best work. He desires for us to let go of control, moving to the passenger seat and letting Him drive. He wants us to learn to let go of our will and replace it with His will. And ultimately He wants to prepare us for the letting-go process that comes as our children someday enter adulthood.

A Friend Who Understands

You and I have covered a lot of ground together. We've looked at Jesus from an angle that is rarely considered. We've dug into God's Word, considered truth, and examined our heart in the process. The Bible tells us that any time we come in contact with God's truth, we will be changed in some way: "So will the words that come out of my mouth not come back empty-handed. They'll do the work I sent them to do, they'll complete the assignment I gave them" (Isaiah 55:11 MSG).

You didn't pick up this book by chance. God planned for you to read it, learn more about who He is, and grow in a closer relationship with Him. He longs for you to know the extent of His love, the expanse of His grace, and the breadth of His forgiveness. He desires for you to know more about who Jesus is so you can grow to be more like Him. He wants you to trust Him with your hopes, your dreams, and ultimately with your life, recognizing that He only wants what's best for you and that He has a heavenly perspective. And He wants you to share what you have learned with your children, giving them an accurate picture of the Savior who loves them even more than you ever could (can you believe that's possible?).

I leave you with these words from Hebrews: "Now that we know what we have—Jesus, this great High Priest with ready access to God—let's not let it slip through our fingers. We don't have a priest who is out of touch with our reality. He's been through weakness and testing, experienced it all—all but the sin. So let's walk right up to him and get what he is so ready to give. Take the mercy, accept the help" (4:14–16 MSG).

You and I have not only a Savior who died for us and a Lord who longs to lead us, but we have a Friend who understands.

Discussion Guide

*H*earts at Home is an organization built on the premise that mothers mother better when they're not alone. Because of that, most of our printed resources are designed to be used either individually or as a group study. If you choose to read this book along with other moms, your discussions will help you process what you read and find application to your own life.

Whether you are a group of two or a hundred and two, a discussion guide can help guide your conversation after you read each chapter. My hope is that it will give you the tools to lead a successful dialogue as your group reads this book together. If you don't know where to start, we've given you a template with which to work. If you are an experienced leader, this section can serve to enhance your own ideas.

Regardless of whether you meet in a living room or a church building, the most important aspect of gathering together is intentionally building relationships. You'll notice that each chapter has a consistent format for discussion. Each section serves a purpose in relationship building. Let's take a quick look at the four elements in the discussion.

Icebreaker

When a group first gets together each week it is beneficial to start out with a lighthearted, get-to-know-you-better activity. The icebreaker time is designed to focus everyone in on the group, the people around them, and the topic at hand. It fosters relationships and builds a sense of camaraderie.

You won't want to spend a large amount of time on the icebreaker; just 10–15 minutes is all it takes to pull everyone together and spend some time laughing and sharing.

After everyone has had the chance to participate in the icebreaker, open your discussion with prayer. Commit your time to the Lord and ask Him to lead your conversation.

Dig Deep

These questions are designed to facilitate discussion. The best groups are not led by a leader who likes to hear herself talk, but rather by a leader who likes to hear others talk. Dig Deep is likely to take anywhere from 20–45 minutes.

If you are leading the discussion, you'll want to familiarize yourself ahead of time with the questions. Jot down additional questions you might present to the group. Create a list of items you need to remember to bring to the meeting. Make sure you pray for the women in your group and for God's guidance as you lead the discussion.

During the group's discussion time your job will be to draw out the women. Inevitably you will have some women who talk easily in a group and others who rarely share. One of your jobs as the leader is to draw out the quieter woman. Don't be afraid to ask her some questions specifically to help her join the discussion. If someone tends to monopolize the conversation, keep the discussion moving by calling on someone else immediately when you pose a question. If the group occasionally gets off the subject, simply pull the focus back to the original question posed to get back on track.

Apply

This section is designed for personal reflection and goal setting. This time helps the reader take all the information she's read and determine what one "nugget" she is going to own. This is the application to daily life that moves us to action. This part of the discussion will take anywhere from 5–15 minutes to complete. If you want to hold one another accountable to make the changes God is impressing upon you as you read together, this is where that will happen, as well.

Pray

You can choose to have one person close in prayer or have a group prayer time. Either will work just fine. Prayer can be both exciting and intimidating depending on a person's understanding and experience with prayer. If the moms in your group are comfortable praying together, take some time at the end of your group to pray together about the things you have learned. As the leader, take the responsibility of closing out the prayer time when the group is finished praying or when the clock requires that you end your time together.

If your group is not comfortable praying together, then close the group in prayer yourself or ask another member of the group who is comfortable praying aloud to do so. Pray whatever God lays on your heart to pray. Remember, there is no right or wrong way to express yourself when it comes to prayer—you simply talk to God as you would talk to a friend.

If you feel more comfortable, you can pray the prayer at the end of each chapter.

Assignments and Notes

In some of the chapters you may find an assignment for the next week or notes to help in your planning. These will help you prepare for the next discussion.

You might want to create a study basket specifically for keeping items you will need each week. Pens, highlighters, index cards, notebook paper, and your copy of the book would be basic essentials. When special items are needed for a specific week, just drop them in the basket and you'll be assured to remember them!

It is a core value of Hearts at Home to provide resources and curriculum to moms, moms groups, and moms group leaders. We hope this book provides you the opportunity to interact with other moms who understand what your life is like. May you grow your friendships with one another and with Jesus Christ as you explore this book together!

Introduction: You Are Not Alone

Ask the moms to read the introduction, "You Are Not Alone," before your first meeting.

The first time your group meets is for the purposes of getting acquainted. After explaining how your group will operate (refreshments, child care, start time, finish time, calendar schedule, etc.) explain that each week will have one chapter of assigned reading as well as the "Perspective" story preceding the chapter. The discussion will then apply to the assigned reading and will include an icebreaker question, a few Dig Deep questions, one or two Application questions, and prayer. You might suggest that everyone bring a Bible because they may occasionally need it, and offer to help someone who doesn't have one to obtain her own copy.

Then have each woman share about herself:

- Name, husband's name, years married

- Children's names and ages

- What she does outside of mothering or what she did BK (before kids!)

- One thing she's hoping to get out of this group

Encourage the moms in your group to go to www.HeartsatHome.org and sign up for the once-a-month free e-newsletter. This will keep encouragement coming even after your *Real Moms . . . Real Jesus* study is finished!

Chapter 1: Jesus served

ICEBREAKER: *If you could go to any country in the world, where would you go? Why?*

DIG DEEP:

1. Have you ever thought about motherhood as the "ministry of availability"? In what way does that reframe motherhood for you?

2. How does the concept of talking to God as a friend feel for you? If you're comfortable, share with the group about your experience with prayer up to this point in your life.

3. Do you struggle with receiving someone's help? If so, why do you think it's difficult for you to allow someone to serve you?

APPLY:
Identify one "takeaway" for this chapter that you want to move from your head to your heart. If you're comfortable, share that with the group.

PRAY

ASSIGNMENT FOR NEXT WEEK: Have everyone bring pictures of themselves in high school.

LEADER: Bring index cards and markers for next week's discussion.

Chapter 2: Jesus worshiped

ICEBREAKER: *Spend time looking at each other's high school pictures and briefly talking about your high school experience. What are three words to describe that season of your life?*

DIG DEEP:

1. Share two or three things that can easily become false gods that you unknowingly worship.

2. Share some victories you had this week in worshiping God with your life and actions.

3. Make a list of mom responsibilities that are an act of worship when done with a right heart. Identify one or two tasks on the list that you struggle doing with a right heart. Commit to pray for one another in each one's identified struggles.

APPLY:

1. What is one "addiction" you can identify that you know you need to give to God? (See page 36–38 for the author's examples.)

2. Write out this verse on an index card and place it somewhere you'll see it every day:

   "So, my dear Christian friends, companions in following this call to the heights, take a good hard look at Jesus. He's the centerpiece of everything we believe, faithful in everything God gave him to do." HEBREWS 3:1–2 (THE MESSAGE)

PRAY

Chapter 3: Jesus was compassionate and tender

ICEBREAKER: *When you hear the words "compassionate and tender," who comes to your mind? Why?*

DIG DEEP:

1. Is there enough margin (time) in your life to allow you to be empathetic? Is there any way you need to manage your time better to allow yourself the time and energy needed to extend empathy, kindness, and compassion?

2. In what way do you struggle owning your own stuff and confessing to God? Why?

3. Identify two ways that you can be intentional about self-care so that you will have the physical and emotional energy to be tender, gentle, and compassionate with those dearest to you.

APPLY:

Watch for the "God appointments" this week. They will probably come at the most inopportune moments, but if you'll yield to God, put on your listening ears and extend kindness, you'll receive an incredible blessing in your obedience.

PRAY

ASSIGNMENT: Next week you will share one piece of trivia about yourself with the group. Be thinking about what you can share.

LEADER: Bring index cards to the next meeting.

Chapter 4: Jesus was angry

ICEBREAKER: *Give each mom an index card and have her write one piece of trivia about herself on the card. Fold the cards in half and collect them in a bowl. Draw one card at a time, read the trivia aloud, and have the moms guess whose card it is.*

DIG DEEP:

1. Can you identify your passion and purpose as a mom? Share your thoughts with the group.

2. Of the twelve steps the author offers in the "Learn to Say No" section, which step do you struggle with the most?

3. Share a couple of "love fences" you have put in your life. Encourage one another in the healthy boundaries you've each set.

4. On the spectrum below, place a dot that represents where you are in reference to being a God pleaser or people pleaser. Are you happy with that? Why or why not?

   God Pleaser ←———————————————→ People Pleaser

APPLY:

What is one area of your life where you'd like to establish more healthy boundaries?

PRAY

ASSIGNMENT: If the group dynamics allow this, pair each mom with another mom who will serve as a prayer partner for the remainder of the study. Ask each mom to pray this week for her prayer partner's specific desires for establishing healthy boundaries in some part of her life.

Chapter 5: Jesus sacrificed

ICEBREAKER: *What is your favorite thing to do once you get your kids in bed at night?*

DIG DEEP:

1. Discuss the concept of the "entitlement generation." As moms, how can we help our kids be others-centered rather than self-centered?

2. Is sacrifice easy or hard for you? Why?

3. Which word describes you better: martyr or mother? Why?

APPLY:

Using Ralph Waldo Emerson's quote: "Good manners are made up of petty sacrifices," pay attention to the petty sacrifices you make in one day. Each time you notice one, thank God for His example of sacrifice and how sacrifice helps you die to yourself.

PRAY

Chapter 6: Jesus forgave

ICEBREAKER: *What interests or hobbies do you have that you pursue or would like to pursue?*

DIG DEEP:

1. Is the concept that forgiveness is a choice a new concept for you? What experience have you had with having to choose to forgive?

2. When you are wrong, what is your default response?

   a) Admit your mistake and ask for forgiveness

   b) Get angry and defend your actions

   c) Try to blame someone else

   d) Are you kidding? I'm never wrong!

3. How do you feel about your default response?

4. The author talks about coming to a Y in the road where you face the choice to get angry or choose to forgive. Share a time when you faced that Y and tell about the choice you made.

APPLY:

Is there anyone you need to forgive? Is there anyone you need to ask for forgiveness? Take this week to clean up any relational messes with the choice of forgiveness.

PRAY

LEADER: Bring index cards next week.

Chapter 7: Jesus taught

ICEBREAKER: *What is one of your favorite memories from grade school, junior high, or high school?*

DIG DEEP:

1. Have you ever considered the idea that home is the place where spiritual training should take place? Have you considered that the church's job? How do you feel about being your child's primary spiritual teacher?

2. Do you have a favorite parable in the Bible? If so, which one? Why is it a favorite?

3. Think of a parenting challenge you are facing. Share your challenge with the group and then discuss ways you can tie God's truth into how you'll lead your kids through this challenge.

APPLY:

Play the "truth or lie" game yourself this week. When watching television, reading a magazine, or listening to the radio, identify if the subtle messages are telling you truth or a lie. Begin to pay attention to the messages that bombard you throughout the day.

Write out this Scripture on an index card and post it on your bathroom mirror: *"Write these commandments that I've given you today on your hearts. Get them inside of you and then get them inside your children. Talk about them wherever you are, sitting at home or walking in the street; talk about them from the time you get up in the morning to when you fall into bed at night."* DEUTERONOMY 6: 6–7 (THE MESSAGE)

PRAY

LEADER: Bring index cards next week.

Chapter 8: Jesus was confident

ICEBREAKER: *If you had an entire day to yourself, what would you do?*

DIG DEEP:

1. What "sinking sand" things have you tried to build your identity on?

2. Have you ever thought, "Hey, this isn't the life I signed up for"? Where has the reality of your circumstances differed from the dreams you had for your life?

3. When is your spiritual birthday? What was that experience like for you?

APPLY:

Choose three things the Bible says about you (see pages 122–123) and write them on an index card. Place the card somewhere you'll be sure to see it every day.

PRAY

Chapter 9: Jesus was tempted

ICEBREAKER: *If money wasn't an issue, what would be your perfect vacation?*

DIG DEEP:

1. Share a time when you experienced temptation. Did you resist or fall for the Enemy's lies?

2. Were you aware that Jesus experienced temptation? How does that make you feel about Him?

3. Is the concept of spiritual warfare new for you? What are your thoughts about spiritual warfare in your personal life and your family's life?

APPLY:

The author lists several steps for tackling temptation (see pages 142–144). Identify which step you need to pursue more intently and ask your prayer partner to pray for you in making that step more intentional.

PRAY

Chapter 10: Jesus wept

ICEBREAKER: *Pull three items out of your purse and explain how they describe you.*

DIG DEEP:

1. Do you default to what the author calls "positive emotions" or "negative emotions"? How do you feel about that?

2. Share a time when your emotions didn't tell you the truth.

3. After reading this chapter would you characterize yourself as:

   a) too emotional

   b) not emotional enough

   c) emotionally balanced and healthy

4. If you chose a or b, brainstorm with your group ideas to bring more balance to your emotional life.

APPLY:

Answer these questions honestly: Do I use my emotions (nonverbally) to get my way? Do I substitute emotions for words? Do I say that things don't bother me, when they really do? Talk to God about those answers this week and ask Him to help you use your emotions in a healthy way.

PRAY

Chapter 11: Jesus prayeð

ICEBREAKER: *What has been the most valuable thing you've learned from this study?*

DIG DEEP:

1. On a scale of one to ten with one being very uncomfortable and ten being very comfortable, rate your comfort level with personal prayer (praying on your own). What about group prayer (praying with other people)? Is that a place you are content with or a place you'd like to grow in?

2. The author talks about having "snacks" with God and also about having "meals" with God. Which word more accurately describes your prayer life? How do you feel about that?

3. What's the best time of the day for you to have a meal with God?

4. Have you ever had an experience of answered prayer? If so, share your experience with the group.

APPLY:

What is one goal you want to set for yourself in regard to prayer?

PRAY

Chapter 12: Jesus trusted

ICEBREAKER: *If you could meet anyone in the world, who would you like to meet? Why?*

DIG DEEP:

1. What were your thoughts when you read the story at the beginning of the chapter about God providing a car to the author's family? Have you ever considered that God still works miracles today? Why or why not?

2. Have you ever experienced having a front-row seat at watching God work? If so, share a God story with the group.

3. What challenges are you facing now where you need to turn fear into faith?

APPLY:

On pages 198–200, the author gives nine steps for turning fear into faith. Identify two steps that you would like to be more intentional about in your own life. Share those steps with the group or your prayer partner.

PRAY

Chapter 13: Jesus let go

ICEBREAKER: *What has surprised you about motherhood?*

DIG DEEP:

1. Discuss your thoughts about the words submit and surrender.

2. Who's in the driver's seat of your life? Why?

3. What have you learned from this study? In what way has your perspective been changed?

APPLY:

Where do you think God wants you to get out of the way and let Him do His best work? How do you feel about that?

Set up a time for your group to do something fun next week (see a movie, go out to dinner, meet for pie and coffee, for example).

PRAY

A Note from the Author

Dear Readers,

I hope you have found this book helpful in finding encouragement as a mom and in deepening your relationship with God. For more encouragement, I invite you to check out the Hearts at Home Web site and my blog. I'd love to know how *REAL Moms . . . REAL Jesus* has encouraged you personally! Drop me a line if you have a chance:

www.HeartsatHome.org
www.JillSavage.org
e-mail: jill@jillsavage.org

Joining you in the journey,
Jill

HEARTS at HOME

The Go-To Place for Moms

At Hearts at Home, we know moms—what they're feeling, what questions they have, and the challenges they face. We also believe that moms should know that they're not alone.

That's why we're here.

Hearts at Home exists to provide ongoing education and encouragement in the journey of being a mom.

In addition to this book, we offer a free, monthly eNewsletter called *Hearts On-The-Go* as well as daily encouragement including our Heartbeat Radio Program, our Hearts at Home website, blog, and eCommunity. We've even been known to hang out on Facebook and Twitter for those times when moms need a quick pick-me-up!

Each year, nearly 10,000 moms attend Hearts at Home conferences throughout the United States and abroad. Each event blends powerful keynote sessions with relevant, practical workshops that equip moms to be the best they can be.

No matter what season of motherhood you are navigating, Hearts at Home is here for you. Will you join us?

Hearts at Home
1509 N. Clinton Blvd.
Bloomington, IL 61702
Phone: (309) 828-MOMS
E-mail: hearts@hearts-at-home.org
Web: www.hearts-at-home.org
Facebook: www.facebook.com/heartsathome
Twitter: @hearts_at_home

Your *No More Perfect* journey continues online.

Embracing imperfection is tough, isn't it? Whether it's with ourselves, our kids, our spouse or just life in general, it's hard to let the world know that we just don't have it all together.

That's why we've created a website to be a road map for your *No More Perfect* journey. It's a community where you'll find encouragement, connection with other moms and a space where you can just be yourself!

Join us at **www.NoMorePerfect.com** for additional resources (including ways to share information about the books with your friends and materials to use with moms groups or book clubs) and ongoing conversations (you can even share your story!) that will help you let go of imperfect and embrace authentic!

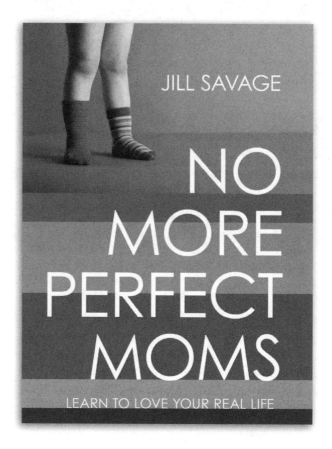

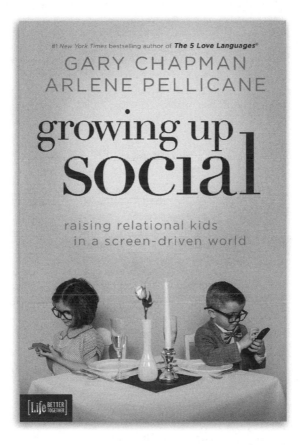

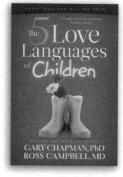

The 5 Love Languages of Children

Not only will Dr. Gary Chapman and Dr. Ross Campbell help you discover your child's love language, but you'll also learn how the love languages can help you discipline more effectively, build a foundation of unconditional love for your child, and understand the link between successful learning and the love languages.

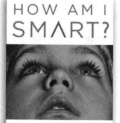

How Am I Smart?
A Parent's Guide to Multiple Intelligences

When parents determine ways children can be smart, they'll better understand their own children's educational needs and how they learn best. This must-read book by Dr. Kathy Koch reveals roots of behavior struggles and relationship conflicts, and their possible solutions. Dr. Kathy unfolds the eight different ways intelligence manifests itself through the "multiple intelligences."

NO MORE PERFECT KIDS
Love Your Kids for Who They Are

One of the best gifts we as parents can give our children is to set them free to be all that God has created them to be—not forcing them to live out our dreams or comparing them to our friend's kid. With encouragement and authenticity, Jill Savage (CEO, Hearts at Home) and Dr. Kathy Koch (Founder and President of Celebrate Kids, Inc.) share inspiration and practical insight for parents everywhere.

Available wherever books are sold.